Master your emotions

Improve your emotional intelligence by controlling your mind and boost your brain to eliminate your anxiety and worry

[Dale Eckhart]

Text Copyright © [Dale Eckhart]

All rights reserved. No part of this guide may be reproduced in any form without permission in writing from the publisher except in the case of brief quotations embodied in critical articles or reviews.

Legal & Disclaimer

The information contained in this book and its contents is not designed to replace or take the place of any form of medical or professional advice; and is not meant to replace the need for independent medical, financial, legal or other professional advice or services, as may be required. The content and information in this book has been provided for educational and entertainment purposes only.

The content and information contained in this book has been compiled from sources deemed reliable, and it is accurate to the best of the Author's knowledge, information and belief. However, the Author cannot guarantee its accuracy and validity and cannot be held liable for any errors and/or omissions. Further, changes are periodically made to this book as and when needed. Where appropriate and/or necessary, you must consult a professional (including but not limited to your doctor, attorney, financial advisor or such other professional advisor) before using any of the suggested remedies, techniques, or information in this book.

Upon using the contents and information contained in this book, you agree to hold harmless the Author from and against any damages, costs, and expenses, including any legal fees potentially resulting from the application of any of the information provided by this book. This disclaimer applies to any loss, damages or injury caused by the use and application, whether directly or indirectly, of any advice or information presented, whether for breach of contract, tort, negligence, personal injury, criminal intent, or under any other cause of action.

You agree to accept all risks of using the information presented inside this book.

You agree that by continuing to read this book, where appropriate and/or necessary, you shall consult a professional (including but not limited to your doctor, attorney, or financial advisor or such other advisor as needed) before using any of the suggested remedies, techniques, or information in this book.

Table of Contents

Introduction 1
Chapter 1: What are emotions 6
   Types of emotions 7
      Anger 12
      Fear/Discomfort 12
      Grief 13
      Happiness 13
      Sadness 14
      Envy 14
      Anxiety 15
      Self-criticism 16
      Frustration 16
      Worry 17
      Disappointment 17
   Emotions and Your Mind 27
   The Nature of Emotions 30
Chapter 2: Constructive emotions and destructive emotions 32
   List of Different emotions 34
   Destructive effects of having an anger problem 38
Chapter 3: What rules your emotions 42
   How Our Thoughts Shape Our Emotions 42
   Success and delaying gratification 44
   Examples of gratification delay 46

Stop drop technique 47

Self-mastery is the master key 49

Impulse control and delayed gratification 49

   ☐ Find ways to distract yourself from temptations and eliminate triggers 51

   ☐ Make spending money difficult 51

   ☐ Avoid 'all or nothing' thinking 52

   ☐ Make a list of common rationalizations 52

Chapter 4: Factors affecting emotions and your mood 53

Sleep 57

Sports 58

Food and drinks 58

Music 59

Relationships 59

   Four Things You Need to Know 60

   Seven Competencies 61

Work environment, ... 63

Words that we use 64

Positive/negative thoughts 64

Chapter 5: How negative emotions affect your health 65

Chapter 6: How positive emotions affect your health 70

Chapter 7: How to change your emotions 74

Why do emotions often take control of people? 74

   People don't Recognize Own Emotions as a Staging Ground 74

   People don't know how to control feelings 75

   People don't understand the impact of Emotions 76

Change your behavior and your bad habits 77
    Denial...77
    Being Overly Serious...77
    Going through Your Phone in the Middle of a Conversation 78
    Calling the Names of the Important People You Know 78
    Subtle Bragging...79
    Screaming at People 79
    Gossiping 79
    Talking a Lot More Than Listening..80
    Posting Too Much of Yourself on Social Media...............................80
    Saying Too Much of Yourself Too Early in a Relationship 81
    Being Closed-Minded...81
    Avoidance 81
    Social Withdrawal 82
    Compulsive Behavior 82
    Self-Destructive Behavior...83
Change your environment to change... 83

Chapter 8: How to deal with negative emotions 85

5 proven strategies and/or therapies to eliminate negative emotions and thoughts... 87
    Develop self-awareness 87
    Listen without judging..90
    Mind-Body Connection 91
    Develop self-management..94
    Learn to cope with criticism...94

5 techniques to control the most important emotions such as fear, worry, panic, forgiveness, anger 96

    Observe Your Feelings throughout the Day 97

    Practice Deep Breathing and Mindfulness 98

    Question Your Perspective 99

    Celebrate Positive Emotions to Attract More of Them 100

    Know Yourself like No One Else 100

Chapter 9: How to read emotions 102

    Create a Room in Your Life for Joy! 105

    How to Condition Your Mind for Better Emotions 109

Chapter 10: How to use your emotion to grow 111

Chapter 11: The key to control emotions 114

    How culture impacts emotions 120

Chapter 12: Famous and motivational speeches 123

    The Signature Symbol 128

        FDR's Invisible Wheelchair 129

    Power Accessories 130

        Maggie's Handbag 130

Conclusion 132

Introduction

If you are currently reading this, it means you are one of the people striving so hard to get rid of anger, stress, and anxiety in order to build a life of positivity for themselves. Well, count yourself lucky because you have just found your one-stop-shop to everything you need to know about anger, stress, and anxiety management; you can now find out everything you need to know about overcoming negativity. The book, "Master your Emotions" contains genuine information, tips, strategies, and techniques that can help you create that happy, negativity-devoid, and quality life you desire and as well, deserve. The book is written in simplified and easy-to-digest language to help you assimilate everything contained within smoothly.

The book will teach you all you need to know about stress management, anxiety management, and anger management by making you privy to some of the most effective techniques and strategies for mastering your emotions and learning emotional intelligence. This book will begin by explaining all the basics you need to know about emotions; the nature of emotions; and the sources of emotions. What impacts our emotions? How are emotions developed? Are negative emotions even necessary at all? How can you get rid of them? These and many more are the questions you will be finding valid answers to in "Master your emotions: improve your emotional intelligence by controlling your mind and boost your brain to eliminate your anxiety and worry."

We will also take an in-depth look at what emotional intelligence is and how it can help you rid your life of negativity. Most importantly, you will learn about anger management and core relaxation strategies to get rid of worries, concerns, and uncertainties. To further help you, we will be giving you tips on how to practice mindfulness meditation which is a popular form of meditation now being used to practice self-awareness. Mindfulness meditation technique can help you develop your connection with your inner self so that you can develop high emotional intelligence.

If you are interested in leading a value-laden life, qualitative, and filled with positivity; if you want to learn to project positivity into negative emotions and you would like to learn how you can be more productive, purposeful, and positive in life but you don't know where to begin from, this one-stop-shop for positivity promises to teach you these and everything else you need to know. Every answer you need awaits you in this amazing read.

The choice is now left to you to choose a life devoid of stress, anger, anxiety; a life of positivity; and start living life with a de-cluttered and free mind using the strategies, tips, and techniques waiting for you in the book. Add a copy to the cart and get started on the journey to positivity and productivity!

However, it wasn't until 1995, when Daniel Goleman published his book by the same name, that emotional intelligence rolled into the mainstream consciousness and became a ground-breaking concept. Back then, intelligence quotient was seen as the only factor that mattered when it came to assessing an individual's capabilities. Once emotional intelligence took over, IQ was perceived as a narrow or limited way of assessing an individual's chances of success. The cutthroat world of career, jobs, and business was starkly different from the cushy confines of a classroom.

If one had to navigate the real world, they'd have to adapt to a different kind of intelligence than the academic one used in classrooms or libraries. A person's knowledge and cognitive abilities alone didn't guarantee success in life. A degree didn't automatically mean a high paying job or a profitable business.

At best, you'll get your foot through the door. However, for someone to succeed, you would need much more than just plain intelligence. It would take social, communication, conversation, and emotional skills to raise the bar. These are life skills that don't come in the classroom but are learned by living in a hostel, waiting at bars, joining social clubs, being a part of sports teams, and volunteering.

Do you still think IQ is the only factor that determines a person's overall success in life? If that was true, my friend, every successful person you spot today from the CEO of big organizations to the president, to thought leaders, and successful entrepreneurs should be a Harvard, Stanford, MIT graduate with a Ph.D.

Make a list of ten successful people you admire the most. They are the people you look up to as they lead successful and balanced lives.

Are all these folks top honors graduates from distinguished educational institutions with a high IQ? My money is on 'No!'

Again, don't get me wrong here. I am not undermining the importance of intelligence or asking you to shut that book on mechanical engineering and start reading about human psychology. It is awesome if you possess naturally high cognitive abilities and a high intelligence quotient. All I am saying is, you should ideally have both EQ and IQ complementing each other to increase your chances of success in the real world. If you can increase your emotional quotient to back up an already high intelligence quotient, you can achieve many great things!

However, if you ask me to pick between two skills, I would have to go with emotional intelligence. A person with average intelligence and highly evolved emotional intelligence has a greater chance of succeeding in today's world than a person with high intelligence and less developed emotional intelligence. The name of the game today is about managing people, understanding their emotions or motives, and managing their feelings to achieve the most positive results.

Technical knowledge may help you direct or instruct your team when it comes to completing a task. However, your ability to keep them motivated by understanding their emotions will ensure they'll stay inspired and productive throughout the process.

A person's cognitive intelligence or intellectual potential has always been measured as his or her ability to retain facts or make calculations. However, these skills aren't necessarily all-encompassing in certain positions such as leadership and entrepreneurship. Tons of CEOs, world leaders, and Fortune 500 company founders are high-school dropouts. If intelligence alone was the measure of a person's success, how would you explain this?

The reality is that it isn't as straightforward as a single factor like intelligence that determines our success. It is, in fact, a combination of factors which are mainly emotional and social life skills that will help you survive or thrive in the real world. Intelligence quotient is an inborn, but not all-inclusive, factor that can influence an individual's success in life.

This is good news because, irrespective of your traditional, genetically determined intelligence, you have a good chance of being successful if you work on other social-emotional life skills. A high emotional quotient along with other social and psychological skill sets can definitely boost your chances.

Chapter 1: What are emotions

Understanding the nature of emotions and what emotions are is the first step to learning how to successfully master your emotions. After all, how could you master something if you don't even know what it is or how it works? In a simpler definition, the Oxford dictionary says emotion is "a strong feeling deriving from one's circumstances, mood, or relationships with others." From both definitions, you can already tell that emotions are related to feelings in a way. However, emotions and feelings are not entirely the same. Human emotions are usually triggered by changes in a person's physiological and behavioral makeup.

As humans, we can usually tell our emotional state at every point. You know when you are feeling happy, sad, or angry. However, what you probably cannot tell is where exactly these feelings originate from. Usually, most of us make the mistake of regarding emotions and feelings as the same thing. We even use both interchangeably in the form of synonyms. But, like we have said; emotions and feelings are two different things that are somewhat dependent on each other. While emotions originate from a subconscious and physiological state, feelings are mostly subjective to experiences and they originate from a conscious state. Emotions may be regarded as automatic bodily reactions to internal or external triggers. Therefore, we can say that there may be emotions without feelings but there can be no feelings without emotions. Feelings are subjects of our emotional state.

Types of emotions

Every emotion humans experience has four important components which are: cognitive, behavioral, physiological, and affect reactions. When you experience an emotion, it is usually triggered and fueled by any of these four components.

Firstly, cognitive reaction to emotions refers to how a person thinks, stores information and experiences, and perceives an event. Behavioral reactions have to do with how humans primarily express an emotion. Physiological reactions on the other hand are triggered by changes in a person's hormonal level. Finally, affect reactions signify the state of emotion and the nature of the emotion itself. Each aspect of emotions as explained usually triggers the other. For instance, let's say that an aunt you don't like comes to visit your parents; immediately you see this person, you automatically think in your mind that she is annoying or scary probably due to past experiences with her and her disposition (this is a cognitive reaction). Due to this perception you have of your annoying aunt, you become grumpy (this is the affect reaction). Then, your parents come to tell you that your aunt will be staying in the house for a while; you feel your blood rising in anger (this is a physiological reaction) and you angrily leave for your room (behavioral reaction). To understand the different components of emotions, you must ensure you know where emotions originate from. Experts have tried to identify the source of emotions using different theories. These theories try to explain the processes of emotions formulation, the sources of emotions, and the cause. We will be looking into these theories, although not in-depth. We will try to understand how emotions occur solitarily.

In the bid to explain emotions, researchers have formulated different theories which are classified under three main categories. We have the physiological theories which propose that emotions are the results of certain responses within the body; there are the neurological theories which suggest that certain activities that take place in the brain are responsible for our emotions; finally, there are theories under the cognitive class which believe that our thoughts, perceptions, and mental activities are responsible for the formulation of emotions.

The first theory that tries to explain emotions is the "evolutionary theory of emotion" which was proposed by Charles Darwin, a naturalist. This theory argues that emotions evolve due to their adaptive nature which promotes human survival and reproduction. Darwin also said that humans seek to reproduce with mates due to feelings of love and affection which are products of emotions. He further explained that feelings of fear cause people to recognize and flee from danger. According to Darwin, we have emotions because we need them to adapt and survive in whatever environment we find ourselves. Emotions trigger appropriate responses to certain stimuli in the environment, thereby promoting our chances of survival. To survive in any environment, we have to be cognizant of our own emotions and that of others. However, it is not enough to be aware of emotions, we must also be able to interpret, control, and respond appropriately to a trigger. Being able to correctly interpret our emotions and that of others makes it possible for us to give suitable and appropriate responses to any situation we find ourselves.

Next is the James-Lange theory which is a prominent physiological theory of emotion. This theory was proposed individually by Carl Lange, a physiologist, and William James, a psychologist. The James-Lange theory of emotion argues that emotions are bodily responses which are triggered as a result of the body's physiological reactions to certain events. According to James and Lange, the emotions you produce in response to a physiological reaction caused by a stimuli in the environment is dependent on your interpretation of the physiological reaction. For instance, if you are watching a frightening scene in a movie and you feel your heart start to race, James and Lange believe that you will interpret the physiological reaction (of your heart racing) as you being scared. Then, you conclude that you are frightened since your heart is racing. The James-Lange physiological theory of emotion proposes that your heart isn't racing because you are scared; rather, you are scared because your heart is racing. Therefore, the emotion of fear you are feeling at that point in time is a response to the physiological reaction taking place in your body.

Another prominent theory which seeks to explain the origin and nature of emotions is the Cannon-Bard theory of emotion. This is also a physiological theory but it seeks to directly counter the submissions of James and Lange. Proposed by Walter Cannon and further expanded by Philip Bard, this theory explains that humans experience physiological reactions linked to certain emotions without necessarily experiencing these emotions. For example, your heart also races when you do something exciting such as exercise, not just when you are scared. According to Cannon, people experience emotional responses so quickly that they simply can't be the results of some physical reactions. As an example, when you watch that frightening movie scene, you often start to feel scared even before noticing that your heart is racing or your hands are trembling. Cannon and Bard, in essence, argue that emotional responses and physiological reactions often occur simultaneously to internal or external stimuli.

The Schechter-Singer theory is another theory of emotion which examines emotions from a cognitive perspective. According to this theory, humans first experience a physiological reaction after which they try to identify the cause of this reaction so they can experience it as an emotion. In other words, you react to external or internal stimuli with a physiological response which you then interpret from a cognitive perspective; the result of the cognitive interpretation is what is considered an emotion. The Schechter and Singer theory is quite similar to both James-Lange and Cannon-Bard theory but the main difference is the cognitive interpretation which humans use to label an emotion, according to Schechter and Singer. Like Cannon and Bard, Schechter and Singer also argued that certain physiological responses in the body can result in different emotions.

The Lazarus theory of emotion or Cognitive Appraisal theory as it is also called was proposed by Richard Lazarus and is another theory that takes a cognitive approach. This theory suggests that thinking always takes place before emotion is experienced. According to Lazarus and other pioneers of this theory, humans react to stimuli immediately with thoughts, after which the physiological response and emotions are experienced. This means that your thoughts always come first before a physiological and emotional response. For example, if you are watching a frightening scene in a movie, your mind immediately starts to think that this movie is scary and frightening. This triggers an emotion of fear, accompanied by related physical reactions such as hands trembling, racing heart, etc.

Finally, we have the Facial-Feedback theory of emotion. This theory suggests that emotional experiences are linked to our facial expressions. What this means is that your physical reactions to stimuli have a direct impact on the emotion you experience, instead of being the effects of the emotion. This theory argues that our emotions are directly linked to changes in our facial muscles. For instance, if you force yourself to smile more when interacting with people, you will have a better time at social events. And, if you carry a frown whenever you interact with people at social events, you'd definitely feel an awful emotion.

These are all theories of emotions which experts have proposed over the years. You may wonder why you even need to learn about the theories of emotions just because you want to learn how to control your emotions. To master your emotions, there is one key thing you must first do; understand how emotions occur. If you want to learn to control an emotion like anger, you definitely need to first identify the source of the anger and all the symptoms associated with it. Once you know this, you can easily put a leash on your rage the next time you feel it brewing.

Emotions are an important part of our lives because they have huge impacts on our actions, reactions, decisions, and ultimately, our lives. There may still be a huge cloud of mystery surrounding why humans experience emotions but with the little knowledge available to us, we should be able to understand and manage our emotions effectively.

Anger

Anger is one of the most unwanted emotions, yet it is frequently manifested. One of the causes of anger is when an individual feels entitled to something. For instance, if you feel that you deserve an award, respect, and attention, then you are on the path of attracting anger when you get disappointment. Most people that tend to be temperamental also show low self-esteem suggesting that each disappointment they get makes them think they are destined to be failures. If unmanaged, anger can cost your health, social life, work, and finances.

Fear/Discomfort

Whenever we try something new, we experience anxiety. We are afraid of the unknown. This is why we like to maintain our daily routine and stay within our comfort zones. From our brain's point of view, this makes perfect sense. If our current habits allow us to be safe and avoid any potential threat to our survival (or the survival of our ego) why bother changing them? This explains why we often keep the same routine or have the same thoughts over and over. It is also why we may experience a lot of internal resistance when trying to change ourselves.

Grief

It is important to grieve the loss of someone or something important in your life, but grief can snowball into a debilitating emotion if it isn't managed correctly. If you find yourself overwhelmed by grief, try to be more active. It is easy while grieving to withdraw socially and stop doing productive activities. Force yourself to engage with others and seek the emotional support that you need from the people you are close to. Don't let your life stagnate. Keep practicing mindfulness, exercising, eating right, and everything else that makes you feel good.

Understand that you don't have to feel guilty for moving on from a loss. Just because you have accepted the loss of that thing or person doesn't mean you've forgotten.

Happiness

As one of the most sought after feelings, happiness regards what we wish to feel in an appealing manner. There are numerous efforts and strategies at personal, community, and governmental levels to enhance levels of happiness as it directly impacts the health of people. Happiness, as an emotion, is manifested through body languages such as a relaxed stance, facial expressions like smiling, and an upbeat illustrated by a pleasant tone of voice.

Like any other emotion, the emotion of happiness is largely created by human experience and the belief system. For instance, if scoring sixty marks is regarded as desirable, then a student is likely to feel happy to attain or surpass the mark. If riding in a train with family members is regarded as being happy then an individual that never had that experience might feel happy and eager at the prospect of boarding a train. Fortunately, we can optimize happiness by enhancing our emotional intelligence levels.

Sadness

As an emotion, sadness is a transient emotional state whose attributes include hopelessness, grief, disappointment, dampened mood, and disinterest. There are several ways to manifest sadness as emotion, and these include:

- **Withdrawal from others**
- **Dampened mood**
- **Lethargy**
- **Crying**
- **Quietness**

Envy

Envy commonly happens at the workplace where an employee admires to be accomplished just like the popular colleague. A human entertains and pursues ambitions routinely, and this allowed. The problem starts when one becomes uneasy with the accomplishments of others to the point of being affected mentally and physically; the person is feeling envious. As expected, persons with a feeling of envy will rarely acknowledge that they are manifesting the negative emotion. At the workplace, envy affects an individual negatively. While the limited and occasional form of envy is necessary to spur one to improve and strive for more, it becomes a problem if it is not managed. Feelings of envy are likely to commonly manifest at the workplace as workplaces appraise employees and reward those accomplished ones.

Overcoming envy requires accepting that we have different competencies and different timings. By accepting that there are individuals more qualified than you will help you create room for accepting others to become more successful than you. It is also important to observe that seasoned employees are likely to deliver compared to recruits. Ability to unlearn can help in managing the feeling of envy. As with any emotion, it is not possible to escape from feeling envy, but one can effectively manage the feeling. When the feeling of envy sets in, convince yourself that in one hour, you will shed off that feeling and not react to the accomplishment of a friend or colleague.

Anxiety

Feeling worried is important to enabling one to visualize and plan for the worst-case scenarios. For instance, being worried about passing exams enables you to address the risk of failing by working harder, consulting, or planning for failure as a possible outcome of the test that you took. However, worry becomes a bad emotion when it takes over you and prevents one from routine activities and routine interactions. For instance, when you constantly feel worried about failure making you study until you get burnout then worry as emotion becomes a negative emotion. As earlier on indicated, feelings emanate from human experience and system of beliefs, and this implies that if the society does not accommodate failure, then you will get the emotion of worry. The emotion is manifesting because of past experiences and the current system of beliefs regarding exams and not necessarily about how you feel internally.

Self-criticism

Self-judgment happens when we critic ourselves and found ourselves inadequate. Self-criticism is necessary as a way of self-evaluation and can help one improve performance, social skills, and communication. A fortunate aspect of human beings is that they can reflect over their experiences, detach from their self and evaluate themselves, and speak to oneself. Limited self-judgment can help increase personal accountability, which can increase the professionalism and appeal of an individual at the workplace and in society. However, self-criticism becomes an issue when one gets stuck at it and feels worthless before society.

Frustration

This is when you feel trapped but can't do anything about it. Frustration in the workplace is the most common cause of burnout.

Worry

With so many layoffs, it's natural to be worried about losing your job. However, instead of feeling anxious, try to focus on your job and think about ways of improving your performance, to you make yourself more employable. Nervous people usually have low self-confidence.

Disappointment

Repeated disappointments always negatively affect efficiency and productivity, and if unaddressed, can lead to burnout and high staff turnover.

The key thing about nurturing negative emotions in the workplace be it feelings about your colleagues, management, working environment, salary, or something else is that these feelings are contagious, and this kind of resentment easily spreads and demoralizes others. This is why a negative person is more likely to be fired, if for no other reason than to prevent their negativity and resentment from spreading to others.

Anger is often perceived from the point of a primary emotion but anger may also be a secondary emotion. In fact, anger is often more secondary than primary. Anger is a basic human emotion that is connected with our survival as humans. It is as basic as happiness, sadness, fear, and other elemental emotions. Like stress and anxiety, anger is also connected with the "fight or flight" response of the nervous system; it is meant for your protection and survival. The fight or flight response is usually activated when someone perceives danger; it prepares you to either fight or flee from the perceived danger. However, fighting in this response has evolved from actual fighting to other things. There are situations where "fighting" doesn't mean getting your punch ready; it may be reacting to an injustice by championing a cause for justice.

Contrary to what you have been made to believe, anger is a perfectly normal, usually healthy, and natural human emotion. But, anger can also become destructive when it gets out of control. We all feel anger at some point in time although in varying degree. This is due to the fact that anger is a part of our experiences as humans. Anger usually arises in varying context and is usually preceded by some emotion which could be pain, injustice, dissatisfaction, criticism, and unfairness generally. Usually, anger comes in different range from irritation to rage. Anger in the form of mild irritation may be caused by feelings of stress, tiredness, and anxiety. In fact, humans are likely to become irritated when their basic human needs like food, shelter, and sleep are not being met. We may also be irritated by thoughts and opinions from other people which do not conform to ours.

Often, when anger becomes an emotion we cannot control, it becomes destructive. It can have a massive impact on our personal and work relationship with others but it doesn't stop at this. Anger is also destructive to our health, physically and emotionally. With unchecked anger usually comes stress and when anger becomes prolonged, the stress hormones that come with anger can destroy certain neurons in some part of the brain responsible for short-term memory and judgment. Anger can also weaken the immune system.

As we have said, anger is a basic human emotion necessary for survival so there are times when anger can be positive and not "bad." In fact, anger is not really a "bad" emotion in itself; it becomes bad when we allow it get to us unchecked i.e. when it becomes uncontrollable. No emotion is necessarily bad as long as we are able to master and control these emotions. Anger may sometime be a substitute emotion which is being used to cover up for something like pain, envy, jealousy, etc. There are people who make themselves angry just so they don't have to feel pain. People change their emotions from pain to anger sometimes because it is easier to be angry than it is to be in pain. This may be a conscious or unconscious action.

Anger is usually grouped into several types by experts and for this book, we will be checking out 8 identified types of anger. Knowing the type or source of your anger makes it easier for this anger to be controlled or managed. All types of anger which we will be examining are psychologically based since anger is an emotion of the mind.

- **Righteous Anger:** This is a positive anger that we feel when an injustice has been committed or when we feel a rule has been broken. It may also be referred to as judgmental or moral anger because it is a morally indignant anger that may also arise due to our perception of someone else's shortcoming. This kind of anger usually stems from belief and rules. That anger you experience when you feel that someone's human right has been abused is a righteous anger. However, this sort of anger may assume a morally superior stance which is that you think you are better than some people and that is why you get angry with them; it may also be because you think someone is better than something they have done. Righteous anger may become excessive out of the need to manipulate and control others.

- **Assertive Anger:** Have you ever used your feelings of rage to initiate a social good or positive change? If yes, then this is what we refer to as assertive anger. It is a constructive kind of anger that serves as catalyst for initiating changes aimed at positively altering the state of something. Rather than express anger in form of confrontations, arguments, outbursts, and verbal abuse, people who get assertively angry express their rage in ways that create a positive change around the situation that got them angry in the first place. This is normally done without any form of destruction, distress, or anxiety. Assertive anger can be a really powerful motivator for you.

- **Aggressive Anger:** Also called behavioral anger, this type of anger is usually physically expressed. It is a highly volatile, unpredictable, and out-of-control that may push you to physically attack someone. But, this doesn't mean that this anger always results in harm or injuries. When this anger overwhelms you, it may push you to lash out at the object of your anger or something else nearby like the wall or a photo frame. Aggressive or behavioral anger may have huge legal and personal consequences. Trauma or neglect from childhood may be the root of this type of anger.

- **Habitual anger:** There are times when anger becomes a perpetual emotion due to the fact that you have spent so much time being angry. Habitual anger refers to when you are in a constant state of irritation, dissatisfaction, and unrest such that pretty much everything annoys you. People who have this kind of habitual anger may even get angrier when confronted about their anger or certain situations. The underlying secret behind this kind of anger is that it is always rooted deep in the past and it accumulates over the years probably due to negative experiences. The older you get without managing this anger, the more you feed it.
- **Chronic Anger:** This is a general and dangerous form of anger. It is the absolute and continual resentment of your situation, certain circumstances, people around you and even yourself. It is a form of habitual anger because it is also in perpetuity. Since it is a prolonged experience,

chronic anger often have immensely adverse effects on an individual's mental and physical wellbeing.

- **Passive-Aggressive Anger:** People who try to avoid confrontations and expression of feelings are the ones who usually experience the passive-aggressive type of anger. Passive-aggressive anger has to do with repressing your anger, rage, or fury in order to avoid getting into arguments and confrontations. This kind of anger is often expressed subtly in the form of sarcasm, verbal abuse, mockery, veiled silence, and chronic procrastination. Most people who express anger passively often don't accept that they are aggressive but their actions may have damaging effects on their personal and professional relationship with others.

- **Verbal Anger:** Often, verbal anger is considered to be milder than aggressive or habitual anger but it is just as bad. This anger is a deeply emotional and psychological which has profound effects on the target of the abuse. It comes in form of threats, mockery, sarcasm, yelling, screaming, furious shouting, blaming, and poor criticism. It is often experienced out of annoyance or irritation.

- **Self-harm:** This is a kind of anger directed by oneself at oneself. It goes way beyond depression. For instance, there are people who cut themselves up; this could be them expressing anger because they probably don't like their looks. Self-harm is quite complicated however you should know that it is a very negative emotion which you can't hold in. Self-harm can be a result of so many thing; physical abuse, emotional abuse, neglect, and trauma. It may also be because of repeated disappointments. Rather than expressing their anger towards the person who has wronged them, some people focus the anger on their inner self.

No matter the type of anger you experience, there are some factors which are the major causes of anger. For effective anger management to take place, you must know and address the cause of your anger. So, let's check out some of the known causes of anger.

Factors that Contribute to Anger

There are many factors that contribute to why you get angry apart from the fact that anger is a natural emotion which you must experience. How you react to situations depend on certain factors in life and these factors are the ones that determine the degree of anger you experienced.

The first known factor that contributes how you experience anger is your childhood and upbringing. As children, many people have been taught certain beliefs about anger; they were taught that anger is destructive, bad, and very negative. Individuals who were taught that it is bad to express anger learn not to complain about injustice; they may have also been punished for expressing their anger as kids. So, they learn to keep the anger in till it becomes a long-term habitual problem. Sometimes, they end up expressing their anger in very unhealthy ways due to years of bottling all that emotions in. They may also turn the anger inwards if there are no other outlets. There are also people who have grown up thinking it is okay to be aggressive or violent so they tend to act out their anger aggressively. This may be because they weren't taught how to properly express their emotions or manage them.

Another factor that contributes to anger and how you react to situations is the past experiences you have had. As a child, if you have experienced situations which made you feel angry and resentful in the past but you weren't able to healthily express this anger at the time, you may still be nursing the anger till the present time. For instance, if you have been abused or you have faced trauma in the past, the anger may still be there lurking somewhere in your heart especially if you weren't able to do anything about it then. Of course, this results in you finding some situations particularly difficult and easy to get you angry.

Your anger problem may also be due to circumstances you are presently faced with and not just things you experienced in the past. Current circumstances and challenges may leave you feeling angrier than normal or make you get angry at things and situations that aren't even related. If there is a situation making you angry and you can't do anything about it, you may express the anger at other times under a totally different condition. As an example, if your boss at work makes you angry and stressed out every day but you can't do anything about it since he's your boss, you may express the anger at home rather than at work. For instance, you may get home and lash at the kids or your spouse grumpily or angrily and then blame it on a "long day."

These are 3 of the most influencing factors for what gets you angry and how you react to potentially raging situations.

Anger as a Positive Emotion

As much as we all like to consider anger a negative emotion, it can also be a positive emotion when we react to it the right way; it is also positive as long as we have our anger under control and never let it consume us. When anger is positive, it means it is driving us to do something beneficial; positive anger lays the foundation for changes and developments.

Positive anger is a highly motivating force which compels us to do something we may have thought we couldn't do in the past. Anger fuels our passion and drives us towards our goals no matter the challenges and barriers that seem to be in our way. It is a constructive kind of emotion which infuses us with the energy and motivation needed to get what we want; it can inspire a clamor for social change and justice (think Martin Luther King). Again, when anger is a positive emotion, it pushes us to be optimistic. Now, this may sound odd and impossible to you but it is true. Anger could make you optimistic just like happiness does.

Anger as a positive emotion can also be very beneficial to our relationships. It is a natural emotion and we have to strive to be as natural as possible in our relationships. There is no need to suck it in and repress your anger with a smile when your partner, relative, or friend wrongs you. According to research, anger becomes negative and detrimental to a relationship when you suppress or hide it. When you repress your anger and give a faux smile, you are not letting your partner know what they have done to wrong you so they may keep doing it which doesn't do the relationship good. However, when you express your anger positively and healthily, it strengthens your relationship and the bond you share with your partner. Anger helps you find solutions to whatever problem you have in your relationships.

Anger can also be positive when we use it for self-insight; this emotion is a pretty good tool for examining and looking inwards ourselves. Anger allows us to see our faults and work on them. If you never express your anger, there is every chance that you would never know what you doing wrong to people to get that reaction which triggers your anger. Sometimes, the fault is with you and not the person who made you angry. When you become self-conscious and self-aware, you can find ways through which you can channel your anger to improve your life for the better. Positive anger promotes positive self-change.

Okay, this next one sounds absolutely odd but what if you learned that anger reduces violence? Yes, it absolutely does. We all know that anger is an emotion that is known to precede violence so how can anger even reduce violence? What happens is that when you get angry, it may be a powerful pointer telling you that something needs to be changed or resolved. When you notice this, anger could motivate you to take actions to mediate the situation which could instigate violence if not checked. Take a moment and imagine a world where no one could react to injustice immediately with anger? Yeah, it does seem like a potentially violent world. Also, when someone wrongs us and we express our anger healthily, it may make them take actions to placate us and right the wrong they committed.

Finally, positive anger can be used to get what you want. One thing you should keep in mind at all time though is that anger can only be positively or used positively when it is justifiable. Anger which makes you feel control is not positive and cannot be used to initiate positive developments or changes. This is the kind of anger you'll need the anger management techniques we will be discussing for. Anger management techniques teach you to transform your anger from positive to negative.

Emotions and Your Mind

Your mind is unique. There is no other psychological framework like yours, and you will experience emotions differently than anyone else. Take falling in love as an example. This may feel like weightlessness/lightness, or it may feel as if a million bees are trapped inside your stomach. It may be intense, or it may be subtle. It may be instantaneous, or it may emerge gradually. It is the same with anger, frustration, weariness, and even happiness. Just because you may not experience the same emotion in the same way as another person does not devalue what you are experiencing.

Because no two people will experience the same emotion, in the same way, no definition will be appropriate for every person. For example, two people battling depression may experience very different symptoms. The first may have trouble sleeping, have no appetite, and have no interest in things that were once enjoyable while the second has trouble with sleeping in too long, binge-eating, and intense waves of despair. These two instances of depression will look strikingly different from an external viewer, but both of these sufferers' emotions and experiences are valid and could be identified as depression.

This is why intense emotions like grief affect different people in such disparate ways. Two siblings are facing the loss of a parent, for example, will each deal with it in his or her way. The first may cling to family and friends for support in coping with the intense grief, while the other may become the family comic, cracking jokes to keep everyone smiling while dealing with the sadness in private. Neither of these responses is wrong; they're just different.

The trick is to stop comparing your emotional self to the emotional selves of others. Identifying and defining emotions in one must be a personal affair. When we compare ourselves with others, we end up invalidating our feelings because they don't seem to "match what everyone else is feeling." Your emotions are yours, and they are valid already in the fact that you are experiencing them.

We do not experience every emotion at the same intensity every time, by which I mean emotional intensity, varies depending on what the experience is. For example, you may experience a low-intensity grief after hearing the news that a favorite performer has passed away, but you may experience a much fuller, more intense grief at the loss of a friend or relative.

As low-and mild-intensity emotions tend to be easier to cope with, these are often constructive. You may cry over the loss of that beloved celebrity, but these tears would likely be cathartic, granting inner relief through the expression of the emotion. A high-intensity emotion, on the other hand, can be more difficult to face or cope with, causing emotional and psychological distress. The loss of a friend, for example, may cause that much higher intensity of grief, making it difficult to continue with daily life.

Not everyone experiences emotions with the same intensity. Some of us are just designed to feel more intensely than others. If you've ever found yourself overcome with emotion over what was, for others, a mundane situation, then you may be an intense feeler. This is not a bad thing, because it also means you feel positive emotions more intensely, but being an intense feeler may be why you struggle with mismanaged emotions. The higher the intensity, the more difficult emotions can be to cope with.

Let's consider depression as an example. We all experience sadness at some point in our lives because we all deal with dissatisfaction and loss, but severe, high-intensity depression is a debilitating and dangerous emotion. It is natural and normal to become sad after a disappointment or a tragic event, but our general perceptions and thought patterns are typically not severely altered by it. We cope with temporary sadness and then move on with our lives. Depression is not so easy to overcome. It is a high-intensity emotion that can severely affect thoughts, feelings, and behaviors, sometimes without any identifiable trigger. Coping with sadness is a difficult but manageable chore while coping with depression is a long-term and complicated journey.

The Nature of Emotions

Emotions can be tricky. By understanding the mechanism behind emotions, you'll be able to manage them more effectively as they arise.

The first thing to understand is that emotions come and go. One moment you feel happy, the next you feel sad. While you do have some control over your emotions, you must also recognize their unpredictable nature. If you expect to be happy all the time, you set yourself up for failure. You then risk blaming yourself when you 'fail' to be happy, or even worse, beat yourself up for it.

To start taking control of your emotions, you must accept they are transient. You must learn to let them pass without feeling the need to identify strongly with them. You must allow yourself to feel sad without adding commentaries such as, "I shouldn't be sad," or "What's wrong with me?" Instead, you must allow reality to be.

Typically, when someone is described as emotional, this is intended to be taken in a negative light. Emotional people are often regarded as impulsive, difficult to talk to, difficult to work with, unscientific, irrational, loud, or resistant to being spoken to. But this characterization is based on assumptions about emotional people. Indeed, labeling someone as emotional is a simple and almost devious way to neutralize and invalidate someone by immediately labeling them as something which they may or may not be.

No matter how mentally tough you are, you'll still experience sadness, grief, or depression in your life hopefully not at the same time, and not continually. At times, you'll feel disappointed, betrayed, insecure, resentful, or ashamed. You'll doubt yourself and doubt your ability to be the person you want to be. But that's okay because emotions come, but, more importantly, they go.

Chapter 2: Constructive emotions and destructive emotions

Negative thoughts strengthen in intensity every time you react to them. If you feel angry with your kid and react to the anger by yelling at him or her, or if you throw a huge fit in reaction to something demeaning your sibling said to you, you will only feel more upset, remorseful, and frustrated later.

Reacting to something means you pay heed to the very first irrational thought you experience. To illustrate, if you feel a strong urge to quit your job when your boss does not give you the raise he promised, you may actually quit your job without thinking about the implications of this decision.

Similarly, if you feel upset, you are likely to react to that sadness by holding on to it and overthinking that very emotion. You fixate on it for hours, days, and weeks only to understand its implications when it turns into a chronic emotional problem.

To let go of the negativity, stop reacting to the emotion and **make a conscious effort to respond to it**. Responding to an emotion, a negative thought, or any situation means that you do not engage in the very first reactive thought that pops up in your head, and instead, you take your time to think things through, analyze the situation, and address it from different aspects to make an informed decision. If you carefully respond to your emotions and thoughts that trigger negative behaviors, beliefs, and actions, you will get rid of the negativity in your life and replace it with hope, positivity, and happiness. Here is how you can do that:

- Every time you experience an emotion that stirs up a series of negative thoughts in your head, stop doing the task and recognize the emotion.
- Very carefully and calmly, observe your emotion and let it calm down on its own without reacting to it.
- You need to fight the urges you experience at that time to react to the emotion. Therefore, if you are depressed and keep thinking how terrible you are, and you feel the urge to lock yourself in your room, control it by just staying where you are.
- Give your emotion some time, and it will calm down.
- Try to understand the message it is trying to convey to you. If you are angry with yourself for not qualifying to the next round of an entrepreneurial summit and have lost the chance of winning the grand prize of $1 million, observe your anger and assess it. Ask yourself questions such as: Why do I feel angry? What does the loss mean to me? Asking yourself such questions helps you calm down the strong emotion and let go of the negative thoughts you experience during that time. Naturally, when you stop focusing on the intense emotion and the negative thoughts it triggers, and you divert your attention towards

questions to find a way out of the problem, you gently soothe your negative thought process.

- Assess the entire situation in depth and find out ways to better resolve the problem at hand. When you focus on the solution and not the problem, you easily overcome negative thoughts and create room for possibilities.

It will be difficult to not react to a strong emotion, but if you stay conscious of how you feel and behave, and make consistent efforts, you will slowly nurture the habit to respond to your emotions, which will only help you become more positive.

List of Different emotions

Emotions can usually be categorized into two different types. However, these types come in different forms. Some experts categorize emotions into two types: emotions to be expressed and emotions to be controlled. Others categorize emotions as: primary emotions and secondary emotions. One thing common with both classifications of emotions. However, is all kinds of emotions are usually either positive or negative? Whether an emotion is primary/secondary or expressed/controlled, it will either be negative or positive. Often, people believe that positive psychology is centered mainly on positive emotions but this isn't quite true. In truth, positive psychology leans more towards negative emotions because it is more about managing and overturning negative emotions to achieve positive results.

Firstly, positive emotions may be defined as emotions that provide pleasurable experience; they delight you and do not impact your body unhealthily. Positive emotions, as expected, promote positive self-development. Basically, we are saying that positive emotions are the results of pleasant responses to stimuli in the environment or within ourselves. On the other hand, negative emotions refer to those emotions we do not find particularly pleasant, pleasurable, or delightful to experience. Negative emotions are usually the result of unpleasant responses to stimuli and they cause us to express a negative effect towards a person or a situation.

Naturally, we have different examples of emotions groups under positive and negative. But most times, you can't authoritatively state if emotion is positive or negative. In fact, there are certain emotions that could be both positive and negative. The best way to discern between a positive and negative emotion is to use your intuition. For instance, anger could be both, positive and negative. So, the best way to know when it is negative or when it is positive is to intuitively discern the cause and the context of the anger. This book is, of course, going to focus more on negative emotions and how you can embrace them to create positive results for yourself.

Anger and fear are the two prominent negative emotions which most of us erroneously assume we have to do away with. To be realistic, we cannot allow these emotions to rule our lives yet; we must also understand that they are a necessary part of our experiences as humans. It is impossible to say that you never want to get angry anymore; what is possible is to say that you want to control your anger and get angry less. Mastering negative emotions such as anger is about recognizing and embracing the reality of them, determining their source, and becoming aware of their signs so that we can always know when to expect them and how to control them. For example, if you master an emotion like anger, you naturally start to discern which situation may get you angry and how you could avoid this situation.

A list of negative emotions includes;

- Anger
- Fear
- Anxiety
- Depression
- Sadness
- Grief
- Regret
- Worry
- Guilt
- Pride
- Envy
- Frustration
- Shame
- Denial…and more.

Many people regard negative emotions to be signs of low emotional intelligence or weakness but this aren't right. Negative emotions have a lot of benefits as long as we do not allow them to overrun us. You aren't completely healthy if you do not let out some negative emotions every now and then. One thing you should know is that negative emotions help you consider positive emotions from a counterpoint. If you do not experience negative emotions at all, how then would positive emotions make you feel good? Another thing is that negative emotions are key to our evolution and survival as humans. They direct us to act in ways that are beneficial to our growth, development, and survival as humans. Anger, mostly considered a negative emotion, helps us ascertain and find solutions to problems. Fear teaches us to seek protection from danger; sadness teaches us to find and embrace love and company. It goes on and on like this with every negative emotion there is.

When we talk about negative emotions, we don't actually mean negative as in "bad." The negativity we talk about in relation to certain emotions isn't to portray them as being bad but rather to understand that they lean more towards a negative reality as opposed to positive emotions. Negative emotions, without doubt, can affect our mental and physical state adversely; some primary negative emotions like sadness could result in depression or worry. We must understand that they are designed just for the purpose of making uncomfortable. They could lead to chronic stress when not checked, making us want to escape these emotions. What you should however know is that we cannot completely escape negative emotions; we can only master them so they don't affect us adversely. Often, some of these emotions are geared towards sending us important messages. For example, anxiety may be a telling sign that there is something that needs to be changed and fear may be a sign that a person or situation may endanger our safety.

Overall, what you should know is that these negative emotions you experience aren't something to be gotten rid of. Rather, they are meant to be mastered so we can employ them in achieving the high-functioning, full-of-purpose life that we desire and deserve. Just like positive emotions, negative emotions are meant to protect us and serve as motivation for us to live a better, more qualitative life and build/maintain quality relationships with people around us.

Note: Negative emotions in themselves do not directly have any impact on our mental and physical health and well-being. How we process and react when we experience negative emotions is what actually matters to our health.

Destructive effects of having an anger problem

Have you ever heard of the saying "A thought murder a day keeps the doctor away?" This saying is a quite insightful one which refers to how letting yourself feel angry is a healthy thing to do whereas suppressing or denying feelings of anger can have an immensely pathological effect on you. From past experiences, what we have come to know about anger is that it only becomes destructive to you or people around you when it is repressed or let out unhealthily. Anger can have profoundly negative effects on you, your happiness, and people around you. Suppressing your feelings of anger has consequences which are utterly destructive. When you repress your anger, you have the tendency of becoming psychosomatic which could cause real harm to your body. Holding in your anger creates tension in the body and this may cause stress which is a major player in many of the psychosomatic illnesses which we have. Based on research done in the past, there has been substantial evidence to prove that suppressing anger can be the precursor to cancer development in the body and may also inhibit progress even after the cancer has been diagnosed and is being treated.

There are so many effects anger could have on your health. Let's examine some of these effects.

- **Heart Problems:** Anger puts you at great risk of having a heart attack. The risk of having a heart attack doubles whenever you have an outburst of anger. When you suppress your anger or express it through an unhealthy outlet, the effect goes directly to your heart meaning it could lead to heart problems. In fact, a study has shown that people with anger disorders or volatile anger are more likely to have coronary disease more than people who show less signs of anger. However, constructive or positive anger is in no way related to any heart problem. It could even be very good for your health.
- **Weak Immune System:** Getting angry all the time can actually weaken the immune system, making you prone to more and more illnesses as a study has confirmed. Based on a study conducted in Harvard Medical School, an

angry outburst can cause a 6-hour drop in the amount of immunoglobulin A, an antibody responsible for defending the body against infections. Now, imagine if you are always angry; you could really damage your immune system unless you learn to control your anger.

- **Cause Stroke:** You are at a very high risk of having a severe stroke if you are the type who explodes every time. Volatile and habitual anger increases your possibility of developing a stroke ranging from a slightly mild blood clot to the brain to actual bleeding in the brain.

- **Increase Anxiety:** Experiencing anxiety at one point or the other is a normal thing but anger can actually worsen your anxiety if care is not taken. In fact, anger is a primary emotion to anxiety i.e. your anxious feelings may be due to underlying anger problems. Anger increases the symptoms of Generalized Anxiety Disorder (GAD) which is an extreme case of anxiety. People with GAD have higher levels of repressed, internalized, and unexpressed anger which contributes to the development of GAD symptoms; this can be quite destructive.

- **Causes Depression:** Anger increases anxiety which can in turn result in clinical depression. Over the years, many studies have found a link between anger, anxiety, and depression, especially when it comes to men. Passive anger is one of the symptoms of depression; you are constantly angry but too unmotivated to act on the anger.

- **Decreases Lifespan:** Anger results in stress and stress is a very strong suspect when it comes to ill health. Combined with stress, anger can have a really strong effect on your health and it can shorten your lifespan due to the number of health problems it can generate. People who constantly experience repressed anger have shorter lifespans than people who express their anger healthily.

Anger should never be repressed or unhealthily expressed. Instead, you should take active efforts to manage your anger and put it under control so as to avoid all of the negative effects of anger which you have just learned about. Never should you try to stifle or suppress your anger. Suppressing emotions as we have reiterated over the chapters makes it hard to manage them or master them like you should. To start with, pay attention to any feeling of anger you experience and use the information gained to discern where the anger is coming from so that you can use one or more of the anger management techniques we will be checking out below to effectively combat anger problems.

Chapter 3: What rules your emotions

Emotions can be triggered by all sorts of things from people, places, and times of day or even certain objects. How triggers work is that they activate thoughts or memories in our brain and cause us to have physical and emotional responses.

Having emotions is a normal human reaction to our life circumstances, the problem comes when we are unable to evaluate our emotions or consider their impact on our lives. Most people passively accept their emotions; they don't even get to the points we have covered where they choose to identify what the emotion is or what has triggered it.

How Our Thoughts Shape Our Emotions

During the 1960s, social psychologist Walter Mischel headed several psychological studies on delayed rewards and gratification. He closely studied hundreds of children between the ages of 4 to 5 years to reveal a trait that is known to be one of the most important factors that determine success in a person's life, gratification.

This experiment is famously referred to as the marshmallow test. The experiment involved introducing every child into a private chamber and placing a single marshmallow in front of them. At this stage, the researcher struck a deal with the child.

The researcher informed them that he would be gone from the chamber for a while. The child was then informed that if he or she didn't eat the marshmallow while the researcher was away, he would come back and reward them with an additional marshmallow apart from the one on the table. However, if they did eat the marshmallow placed on the table in front of them, they wouldn't be rewarded with another.

It was clear. One marshmallow immediately or two marshmallows later.

The researcher walked out of the chamber and re-entered after 15 minutes.

Predictably, some children leaped on the marshmallow in front of them and ate it as soon as the researcher walked out of the room. However, others tried hard to restrain themselves by diverting their attention. They bounced, jumped around, and scooted on the chairs to distract themselves in a bid to stop them from eating the marshmallow. However, many of these children failed to resist the temptation and eventually gave in.

Only a handful of children managed to hold until the very end without eating the marshmallow.

The study was published in 1972 and became globally popular as 'The Marshmallow Experiment.' However, it doesn't end here. The real twist in the tale is what followed several years later.

Researchers undertook a follow-up study to track the life and progress of each child who was a part of the initial experiment. They studied several areas of the person's life and were surprised by what they discovered. The children who delayed gratification for higher rewards or waited until the end to earn two marshmallows instead of one had higher school grades, lower instances of substance abuse, lower chances of obesity, and better stress coping abilities.

The research was known as a ground-breaking study on gratification because researchers followed up on the children 40 years after the initial experiment was conducted, and it was sufficiently evident that the group of children who delayed gratification patiently for higher rewards succeeded in all areas they were measured on.

This experiment proved beyond doubt that delaying gratification is one of the most crucial skills for success in life.

Success and delaying gratification

Success usually boils down to picking between the discomfort of discipline over the pleasure and comfort of distraction. This is exactly what delaying gratification is. Would you rather go out for the new movie in town where all your friends are heading, or would you rather sit up and study for an examination to earn good grades? Would you rather party hard with your co-workers before the team gets started with an important upcoming presentation? Or would you sit late and work on fine tuning the presentation?

Our ability to delay gratification is also a huge factor when it comes to decision making and is considered an important aspect of emotional intelligence. Each day, we make several choices and decisions. While some are trivial and have little influence on our future (what color shoes should I buy? Or which way should I take to work?), others have a huge bearing on our success and future.

As human beings, we are wired to make decisions or choices that offer an instant return on investment. We want quick results, actions, and rewards. The mind is naturally tuned for a short-term profit. Why do you think e-commerce giants are making a killing by charging an additional fee for same day and next day delivery? Today is better than tomorrow!

Think about how different our life would be if we thought about the impact of our decisions about three to five years from now? If we can bring about this mental shift where we can delay gratification by keeping our eyes firmly fixated on the bigger picture several years from now, our lives can be very different.

Another factor that is important in gratification delay is the environment. For example, if children who were able to resist temptation were not given a second marshmallow or reward for delaying gratification, they are less likely to view delaying gratification as a positive habit.

If parents do not keep their commitment to reward a child for delaying gratification, the child won't value the trait. Delaying gratification can be picked up only in an environment of commitment and trust, where a second marshmallow is given when deserved.

Examples of gratification delay

Let us say you want to buy your dream car that you see in the showroom on your way to work every day. You imagine how wonderful it would be to own and drive that car. The car costs $25,000, and you barely have $5000 dollars in your current savings. How do you buy the car then? Simple, you start saving. This is how you will combine strong willpower with delayed gratification.

There are countless opportunities for you to blow money every day such as hitting the bar with friends for a drink on weekends, co-workers visiting the nearest coffee shop to grab a latte, or buying expensive gadgets. Every time you remove your wallet to pay, you have two clear choices: either blow your money on monetary pleasure or wait for the long-term reward. If you can resist these temptations and curtail your expenses, you'll be closer to purchasing your dream car. Making this decision will help you buy a highly desirable thing in future.

Will you spend now for immediate gratifications and pleasures, or will you save to buy something more valuable in the future?

Here is another interesting example to elucidate the concept of delayed gratification. Let us say you want to be the best film director the world has ever seen. You want to master the craft and pick up all skills related to movie making and the entertainment business. You visualize yourself as making spectacular movies that inspire and entertain people for decades.

How do you plan to work towards a large goal, or the big picture (well, literally)? You'll start by doing mundane, boring; uninspiring jobs on the sets such as being someone's assistant, fetching them a cup of coffee, cleaning the sets, and other similar boring chores. It isn't exciting or fun, but you go through it each day because you have your eyes firmly fixated on the larger goal, or bigger picture.

You know you want to become a huge filmmaker one day and are prepared to delay gratification for fulfilling that goal. The discomfort of your current life is smaller in comparison to the pleasure of the higher goal. This is delayed gratification. Despite the discomfort, you regulate your actions and behavior for meeting a bigger goal in the future. It may be tough and boring currently, but you know that doing these arduous tasks will give you that shot to make it big someday.

Delayed gratification can be applicable in all aspects of life from health to relationships. Almost every decision we make involves a decision between opting for short-term pleasures now and enjoying bigger rewards later. A burger can give you immediate pleasure today, whereas an apple may not give you instant pleasure but will benefit your body in the long run.

Stop drop technique

Each time you identify an overpowering or stressful emotion that is compelling you to seek immediate pleasure, describe your feelings by writing them down. Make sure you state them clearly to acknowledge their existence.

Have you seen the old VCR models? They had a big pause button prominently placed in the middle. You are now going to push the pause button on your thoughts.

Focus all attention on the heart as it is the center of all your feelings.

Think of something remarkably beautiful that you experienced. It can be a spectacular sunset you witnessed on one of your trips, a beautiful flower you saw in a garden today, or a cute pet kitten you spotted in the neighborhood. Basically, anything that evokes feelings of joy, happiness, and positivity in you. The idea is to bring about a shift in your feelings.

Experience the feeling for some time and allow it to linger. Imagine the feelings you experience in and around your heart. If it is still challenging, take deep breaths. Hold the positive feeling and enjoy it.

Now, click on the mental pause button and revisit the compelling idea that was causing stressful feelings. How does it feel right now?

Now write down how you are feeling and what comes to mind. Act on the fresh insight if it is suitable.

This process doesn't take much time (again, you are craving instant gratification) and makes it easier for you to resist giving in to temptation. The real trick is to change the physical feeling with the heart to bring about a shift in thoughts and eventually, actions. You don't suffocate or undermine your emotions.

Rather, you acknowledge them and then gently change them. When your emotions are slowly changing, the brain tows its line which makes us think in a way that lets us act according to our values and not on impulse or uncontrollable emotions.

Self-mastery is the master key

According to Walter Mischel, "Goal-directed and self-imposed gratification delay is fundamental to the process of emotional self-regulation." Emotional management, or regulation and the ability to control one's impulses, are vital to the concept of emotional intelligence.

Mischel's research established that while some people are born with a greater control for impulses, or better emotional management, others are not. A majority of people are somewhere in between. However, the good news is that emotional management, unlike intelligence, can be learned through practice. EQ isn't as genetically determined as cognitive abilities.

Impulse control and delayed gratification

Have you ever said something in anger and then regretted it immediately? Have you ever acted on an impulse or in haste only to regret it soon after the act? I can't even count the number of people who have lost their jobs, ruined their relationships, nixed their business negotiations, and blown away friendships because of that one moment when they acted on impulse. When you don't allow thoughts to take over and control your words or actions, you demonstrate low emotional intelligence.

Thus, the concept of emotional intelligence is closely connected with delaying gratification. We've all acted at some point or another without worrying about the consequences of our actions. Impulse control, or the ability to construct our thoughts and actions prior to speaking or acting, is a huge part of emotional control. You can manage your emotions more efficiently when you learn to override impulses, which is why impulse control is a huge part of emotional intelligence.

Ever wondered about the reason behind counting to ten, 100, or 1000 before reacting each time you are angry? We've all had our parents and educators counsel us about how anger can be restrained by counting up to ten or 100. It is simple, while you are in the process of counting; your emotional level is slowly decreasing. Once you are done with counting, the overpowering impulse to react to the emotion has passed. This allows you act in a more rational and thoughtful manner.

Emotional intelligence is about identifying these impulsive reactions and regulating them in a more positive and constructive manner. Rather than reacting mindlessly to a situation, you need to stop and think before responding. You choose to respond carefully instead of reacting impulsively to accomplish a more positive outcome or thwart a potentially uncomfortable situation.

Here are some useful tips for delaying gratification and boosting your ability to regulate emotions:

☐ Have a clear vision for your future

Delaying gratification and controlling impulses or emotions becomes easier when you have a clear picture of the future. When you know what you want to accomplish five, eight, ten, or 15 years from now, it will be a lot easier to keep the bigger picture in mind if you come across temptations that can ruin your goal. Your 'why' (compelling reason for accomplishing a goal) will keep you sustained throughout the process of meeting the goal. Have a plan to fulfill your goal once you have a clear goal in mind. Identifying your goals and planning how you'll get there will help you resist the temptation more effectively.

☐ Find ways to distract yourself from temptations and eliminate triggers

For instance, if you are planning to quit drinking, take a different route back home from work if there are several bars along the way. Instead of focusing on what you can't do, concentrate on the activities you are passionate about. Surround yourself with positive people and activities that will help you dwell on your goal. Avoid trying to fill your time with material goods.

☐ Make spending money difficult

If you are a slave to plastic money and online transactions, you are making the process of spending money too easy for your own good.

Paying with cold, hard cash can make you think several times before spending. You'll reconsider your purchases when you pay with real money rather than plastic. Take a part of your salary and put it into a separate account that you won't touch. Make sure that accessing your savings account won't be easy.

☐ Avoid 'all or nothing' thinking

Most of us think resisting temptation or giving up a bad habit is an 'all or nothing challenge.' It is natural for a majority of normal human beings to have a minor slip here and there. However, that doesn't mean you should just fall off and quit. Occasional slip-ups shouldn't be used as an excuse to get off the track. Despite a small detour, you can get back on the track. Don't try to convince yourself to wander in the opposite direction.

☐ Make a list of common rationalizations

Find a counterpoint or counterargument for each. For example, you were angry for just five minutes, or you are spending only ten dollars extra. Tell yourself that five minutes of anger is 150 minutes a month wasted in anger or ten dollars extra is $3,000 extra spent throughout the year.

Chapter 4: Factors affecting emotions and your mood

What impacts emotions? This is a valid question to ask if you want to understand and master your emotions. From the context of this chapter, we will be looking at two important things that impact emotions; the brain and social norms/culture.

The brain is a grand master in manipulating emotions so even when you think you know the source of your feelings or emotions, it could be really tricky. We like to think we are in control of our feelings and the triggers behind these feelings, but the truth is our brain has a much more profound impact than people like to admit.

Every single moment, there are lots of activities going on in your head and the brain is at the center of all these activities and somewhat complex processes. A lot of process is involved in how we interpret situations and react to them. Remember that emotions are defined by three important things: cognition, responses, and reaction. The brain determines every of these activities which makes us wonder how our brain actually impacts our emotions. What happens in your brain right before you experience an emotion?

The first thing to know about your emotions is that it starts right from the brain. Emotions are a combination of our feelings, the way we process these feelings, and our responses or reactions to those feelings. The primary purpose of emotion, according to Charles Darwin, is to encourage seamless human evolution. In order for us to survive, we have to pass on our genetic information from generation to generation which is why emotions are important. Recognizing the important of emotional experiences, the brain takes it upon itself to evaluate stimuli and activate a suitable emotional response to it. The brain reflects and considers the best way to respond to a situation so that the primary purpose of survival is achieved and then, it activates a suitable emotion as response so as to propel the rest of the body to react accordingly. So, when you find yourself reacting to a situation with a kind of response, that is actually your brain triggering the emotion it considers right for your survival right at that moment in time.

The brain is a vast network of complex processes which include information processing. One of the brain's primary networks contains neurons which send signals from one part of the brain to the other. Now, these cells or neurons transmit signals through what we call neurotransmitters; some kind of chemicals we either receive or release in the brain. The neurotransmitters are what make it possible for one part of the brain to communicate with another part. Dopamine, norepinephrine, and serotonin are some of the most examined neurotransmitters. Dopamine is the neurotransmitter that has to do with feelings of pleasure and rewards; it is the chemical which makes you happy when you do something good. This neurotransmitter is released as a reward for you to give a pleasurable and happy feeling. On the other hand, serotonin is the neurotransmitter linked with learning and memory. It is believed to play a critical part in brain cells regeneration and research has shown that an imbalance in serotonin can lead to an increase in stress, anger, anxiety, and depression. Norepinephrine on its own helps modify your moods by controlling the levels of stress and anxiety.

Now, when there is an abnormal or unbalanced release and processing of either of these chemicals, there is usually a very profound impact on your emotions and emotional state. For instance, when you do something that requires dopamine to be released and sent to the part of the brain responsible for information processing but your brain doesn't process or receive the dopamine as it should, it could result in you feeling sad or mildly unhappy. Therefore, the abnormal release and processing of dopamine, serotonin, and norepinephrine has immense impact on the emotions you have and the responses you give to certain situations. The next time something which should have made you happy gives feelings of sadness, remember these neurotransmitters.

Again, your brain exerts influence on emotions because it is central to how emotions are formed. The brain consists of different parts that are all responsible for generating different emotions. The part of the brain responsible for processing emotions is the 'emotional brain' which is generally referred to as the limbic system. In this limbic system, we have the amygdala which, as we have said in a previous chapter, helps you measure the emotional quality or value of a stimulus before initiating an appropriate response; it is the part of the brain responsible for initiating the fight or flight response. The hypothalamus helps you regulate your responses or reactions to emotional triggers. There are also other parts of the brain like the hippocampus which all impact your emotions due to its memory retrieval functions. In fact, the hippocampus determines your emotional responses to triggers. Since different parts of the brain process different types of emotions using different methods, damage to any part of the brain can have a huge influence on your emotions and moods no matter how mild. Central to all of this is the limbic system which takes a generalized and simple approach to stimuli.

The brain's left and right hemispheres also play important roles in emotion and responses. The hemispheres are responsible for keeping you functioning but they also play a part in how you process information. The left hemisphere deals more with concrete thinking while the right hemisphere concentrates on abstract thinking. Because they both process information in different ways, the left and right hemispheres work together to manage emotions. While the right hemisphere identifies an emotion, the left hemisphere interprets the emotion. For instance, when the right part of the brain identifies an emotion like anger, it alerts the left brain which then makes a logical decision in interpreting the context of the emotion and deciding the appropriate response to give. This is actually all a synchronized system but if something goes wrong and one hemisphere can't do its job properly, it affects how you react to basic emotions. For example, if the right brain doesn't identify a negative emotion like it should, it prompts the left brain to become overwhelmed with the emotion without knowing how to respond.

Memory whether long-term or short-term is the function of the brain and our memories dictate and inform our emotions. You get angry when you recall a resentful memory and get happy when you remember a pleasant memory. This is a continual process in the brain; it identifies a past emotion and then places you in a mood based on the emotion. So, when next you get angry without knowing why, it may be your brain recalling some painful memory to initiate a negative emotion. How you can override this is to push yourself to think of things that have made you happy in the past. For example, if you are sad, simply thinking of some happy memories can trigger the release of dopamine which rewards you with feelings of happiness.

Sleep

When do you struggle with sleep the most? It is probably the times you had so much on your mind, and rest seemed to be a far-fetched idea. Anxiety and negative emotions can cause a person to become restless, and this has adverse effects on sleep patterns.

Quality sleep is one of the prerequisites for a healthy body, and when your body is deprived of sleep, it can create a ripple effect that affects you mentally and physically. Sleep loss affects your attention span. You will realize over time that you don't pay enough attention to your work or what others say to you.

Sleep deprivation also prevents the body from strengthening its immune system with the cytokines needed to fight infection. When you don't have enough cytokine in your body, it will take a longer time for you to recover from illnesses.

Anxiety, worry, fear, panic attacks, and sadness are some of the negative emotions that affect your ability to sleep peacefully daily. If you don't find a way to manage such feelings, you will be dealing with more problematic health and physical issues.

Sports

This has been proven to be true over a series of studies. So, if you want to put your feelings in check, stay away from junk food, eat balanced meals, and maintain a good routine of exercise.

Keeping your feelings in check overtime can be tough. This is why many persons do not make much effort and give up eventually. Sometimes, you will lose the plot, but this should not deter you from moving on.

A person who can manage effectively manage his emotions and put his feelings in check will be viewed as one with logical reasoning, an effective conflict handler, a person with high emotional intelligence, inner peace, and self-confidence.

Food and drinks

When a person is dealing with negative emotions, food is usually the last thing on their mind. Not eating may or may not be intentional in that state. But anxiety always paves the way for eating disorders, and this is true because most people who are diagnosed with eating disorders struggle or may have struggled with stress in the past.

Eating disorders are illnesses. The people who experience them observe a sudden change with eating, which is usually caused by their anxiety over weight gain and how they look.

Music

Art is a great way to use non-verbal expression to increase your mental well-being. Art is a magical carrier of emotion for humans; we tend to use art to understand the world and make sense of it. This is not the only function of art, however; there are many functions. One is dancing; others are relaxation, grief, mourning, celebration, and war-rousing. There are many functions of music, and nearly all of them our emotions. Music is a great example of an art form that can transform the emotional experience and bring about emotional awareness. If a person is sad all day, and goes to work, comes home, eats dinner, and watches a movie before going to bed, with no other consideration, they are just keeping that sadness inside. You have to do something about it to deal with emotions, and learning to deal with emotions only learned after a person is able to identify their emotions it is the first step on the path to self-realization.

Relationships

Once you've raised your social awareness skills and learn how to understand what other people are feeling, you are ready to work on maintaining your relationships. Let's clear it from the start – this is not an easy job. You will need to use all other areas of emotional intelligence to help you build and maintain them.

Four Things You Need to Know

The first thing you need to assess and manage is the effect different people have on you, as well as recognize what they are feeling and what is the cause that they are feeling that way. If you fulfill that, you will be able to make a decision on the best way to communicate with them to achieve the result that suits your or their needs.

Four different criteria determine the effectiveness of managing relationships:

- Deciding which course of action is the most appropriate for a given situation. To discover this, you will need to recognize the current feeling of the other party and the reason behind that feeling. You will probably have several choices to interact based on the research you conducted, and each of them will cause a different reaction. You will also recognize and appropriately manage the effect they have on you
- Interacting with the other party based on your research
- The result is what should guide you to choose what to say and how you will communicate your message. That means that your actions come with a particular goal in mind, making managing your relationship an intentional activity

- Your needs will be what will cause you to want a particular outcome. It might be your personal needs or the needs of your business

Seven Competencies

Certain competencies might be best related to workplace relationships, but they can also be applied to relations outside of work. The reason you might primarily connect them to your office is that they have a lot of similarities with leaders.

Goleman defined the competencies, and they include:

- **Influencing** – the ability to persuade other people into doing something that fits your, their, or joint needs
- **Inspiring** – the skill to motivate other people by inspiring them
- **Developing** – the ability to give useful feedback and help others build their knowledge and skills
- **Being a catalyst for change** – knowing when change is required and starting the process
- **Managing conflicts** – the ability to efficiently settle or misunderstanding, differences of opinion, or disputes
- **Creating bonds** – building networks and maintaining them
- **Collaborating with others** – creating effective teams and nurturing them

You can use each of these competencies to maintain your relationships. However, before you do that, take some time to think about them.

The question you should ask yourself is "Do you perform these competencies right now and are you good at them?"

It's always a good idea to write everything down. Think about various areas of each competency and note what you are doing well and what can be improved. For example, providing feedback for other people is something that you surely do right now. On the other hand, you can also write where you could use some improvement (yes, it might be the same competency, just a different area).

The next step is to think of two actions that you will take to develop yourself in that area and write them down. Taking an online course, conducting your own research, reading a book, or trying to mirror the behavior of someone you respect are all included. Finally, try to actually perform these actions and work on your competencies. You will notice that it will improve managing your relationships with others.

Let's take a look at the example of giving feedback. You are already giving it to other people, but you would like to work on it and make it more supportive. You conduct an online research and discover some tips and try to apply them the next time someone asks you for feedback. You will notice that they will more appreciate the feedback that's supportive and constructive and your relationship will benefit from that.

Work environment,

For emphasis, it is not possible to eliminate all difficult situations because of the nature of human interactions and the need to take risks as well as adventure. There are also external factors that are beyond the scope of individual control. Avoiding circumstances that trigger adverse emotions is among the effective ways to condition the mind to handle setbacks. An example is where an individual feels irritated when a deadline is fast approaching. It might help if the person started planning and working earlier by splitting the work into modules. One can go further and inform colleagues that short deadlines may make the person react adversely. Change the environment where possible to get away from triggers, especially where the triggers are non-human entities. The bottom line is to ensure that the mind is prepared and has little pressure when handling a challenging issue.

It is important to learn to change thoughts. It might appear an easy strategy, but most people struggle to let go of their thoughts. As indicated earlier, thoughts impact emotions and subsequently, emotional reactions. The persistence to current thoughts occurs because the mind is trying to solve pending issues, and this is sometimes useful. Through the use of cognitive reappraisal, one can replace adverse thoughts with constructive thoughts. Sticking to negative thoughts could also be linked to low self-esteem.

Words that we use

You cannot take words back, so when you are about to use abusive words in a fit of anger, rest assured they will go a long way to harm the person you are saying them to. You can say you don't mean them later, but the words have already had their effect. Sometimes the use of hurtful words stems from a desire to make them feel the hurt you're feeling, but it's not necessary.

Positive/negative thoughts

The way you interpret different situations is highly influenced by your emotions. When you are excited, you are more likely to view situations with optimism, while sadness brings about fear and pessimism. Reflect on your emotional filter and take a more realistic stance by reframing your thoughts.

Restructuring your thoughts involves embracing a more positive outlook when pessimism sets in. Not all situations will present itself with the same level of ease. Something's, all you need to do to step back, look within, isolate your emotions, so that you can have a clear line of thought. While more is required, the bottom line is to stop ruminating on negativity. You will easily lose control of managing your feelings. You can embark on activities that will switch the channel of negativity in your brain, such as taking a walk and running a chore.

Chapter 5: How negative emotions affect your health

Sometimes, our emotional distress manifests as physical distress, causing negative changes in the body. If you've ever been so stressed out that you found yourself with your nose over a toilet or so angry that your vision begins to go black and blotchy at the corners, then you understand how intense emotions can make us feel physically ill. Perhaps, you've had chronic stomach pain for years, but no doctor has been able to tell you why because the cause is not physical but psychological. This could be because it is your emotions causing your pain and not a physical ailment.

A common physical symptom of poor emotional health is a change in appetite. Many people who are suffering from depression experience a loss of appetite and subsequent weight loss. The body still gets hungry because it needs fuel to function, but even favorite foods may become flavorless and unappetizing. Sugar, though, affects the brain's pleasure center, which craves the good feelings sugary foods cause. This may explain why people with depression sometimes gain weight and struggle with binge-eating.

Another common physical manifestation of intense negative emotion is digestive problems. The brain and the digestive tract communicate with each other all the time, which is why you may become nauseous when nervous. When you experience intense emotional distress, it causes disruptions in the natural contractions of your bowels. It also lowers immunity, which makes it easier for infection to take hold within the digestive tract.

You're Body on Anger

Anger itself is not always negative. It alerts us to something or someone in our life that is not right and motivates us to correct that and express our frustration. Incessant anger and rage, however, can be damaging to your physical health.

Chronic or mismanaged stress and anger can cause discomfort in the body and damage to personal health in a variety of ways. Here's a list of common physical symptoms caused by negative stress and anger:

- Accelerated heart rate
- Accelerated breathing rate
- Increased blood pressure
- General aches and pains
- Muscle tension and pain
- Jaw clenching/teeth grinding
- Stomach/digestive issues
- Lowered immune function
- Difficulty healing
- Dizziness and nausea
- Insomnia or trouble sleeping too much
- Loss of or increase in appetite
- Loss of sex drive

- Tinnitus/ringing in ears

Eczema and other skin conditions

Stress and anger are not the only emotions that can cause you physical distress. Depression can wreak as much havoc with your physical health as it can on your emotional health, causing an array of symptoms and worsening existing conditions. Many people experience the physical symptoms of depression but may not realize that these symptoms have a psychological cause, which makes finding solutions to these physical issues much more difficult.

Impact of Negative Emotions on Health

Aside from stomach challenges, negative emotions have several other health implications. There are illnesses and health issues you've had in the past that you thought were a result of diseases but were caused by your overindulgence on toxic energy.

Heart Health

Negative emotions have the same kind of impact that stress has on the heart. When you are anxious, you tend to want to do a series of things that will help you feel better. Some of these things may not be healthy for you as they include reliance on alcohol, smoking, or overeating comfort food.

Eating Disorders

When a person is dealing with negative emotions, food is usually the last thing on their mind. Not eating may or may not be intentional in that state. But anxiety always paves the way for eating disorders, and this is true because most people who are diagnosed with eating disorders struggle or may have struggled with stress in the past.

Eating disorders are illnesses. The people who experience them observe a sudden change with eating, which is usually caused by their anxiety over weight gain and how they look.

Unplanned Weight Loss

Anything toxic will affect you emotionally and physically; it will become evident that you are going through something, and one of the physical manifestations is weight loss. Yes, we all want to maintain a proper and healthy weight, but unplanned weight loss can be terrible, especially when you are also dealing with eating disorders.

Your clothes will no longer fit properly. You will look exhausted and unhealthy, which will also cause people to ask a lot of questions. Even if you weren't a very chubby person before this challenge, the amount of weight you shed would be too obvious to ignore.

Unplanned weight loss can also affect a person's psychology because if you don't understand the connection between your emotions and weight loss, you will start to think you are very sick. Some people go to the doctor, hoping to get diagnosed for an illness they don't have.

Toxic emotions have a way of making you put the source of your worry ahead of yourself; you no longer take care of yourself or put your well-being first. In most cases, some people realize that they've lost weight after a long time because they weren't paying attention to their bodies.

Unhealthy weight loss will make you susceptible to illnesses and fatigue. You will always feel tired, and this can lead to unproductivity with everything you do. It is quite amazing to think that all these health problems started with just one wrong idea. So does this mean we can reverse the process with positive thinking?

Chapter 6: How positive emotions affect your health

When you feel good, everything else feels excellent, even your health. If you take the time to compare and contrast the state of your health when you felt anxious and when you weren't, you would agree that you felt healthier when you were happy.

But aside from the "feeling" of being healthy, it is a fact that positive emotions have an excellent effect on mental and physical health — people who are happy fall ill less often compared to those who are anxious or depressed.

Because of the impact of positive moods on health, there is a new term known as "positive psychology," which entails the use of different techniques that encourage us to identify and develop positive emotions for better health experiences.

Positive psychology emphasizes the fact that attention should be placed on problem-free emotions while urging individuals to concentrate more on their strengths and not on their weaknesses. Anxiety is often a result of speculations about the worst-case scenario and fixating attention on the things you cannot do while anticipating disappointing results.

But with positive psychology, you are encouraged to look beyond the fear that causes you to have eating and sleeping disorders. You are also empowered to build the best things in your life and repair the worst.

As an individual, you need to thrive, and this also means you need to be in good health to achieve that, but good health is connected to your emotions, which takes us right back to the healing ability of good feelings.

If you are having trouble sleeping because you are anxious, try to be happy and worry less. You will notice that your sleep patterns will improve. If you love yourself above everyone else and appreciate your body, you wouldn't have issues with eating disorders or be anxious about how you look.

Being healthy isn't the absence of illness, and that is what positive psychology seeks to express fully. In addition to being free from diseases, your newfound optimism will help you enjoy good heart health. It will cause you to enjoy a long and happy life where you aren't pressured to become anything other than what you are.

We are not concerned about the idea of longevity, which is all about how long we'll live. We are concerned with the impact and quality of life we have, which is what matters. However, the good thing about this thought process is that, while you aren't precisely focused on how long you'll live, if you do enjoy positive emotions, having a long life will surely be in the cards for you.

What Takes Place in Your Brain When You Are All about Positive Emotions?

Negative emotions cause you to be completely fixated on the cause of your anxiety, which also makes it difficult for you to be 100% aware of the other good things you have going for yourself. Sadly, the more narrow-minded you are with the problem, the more damage it does to your health.

The headaches you feel most times are because you find some things very complicated and challenging to handle, but when you have more positive emotions, stressful situations will be easier to handle. The ideas you labeled as "complex" will become easy because positive emotions help you build emotional resilience.

We will talk more about emotional resilience in another chapter, but what you should know now is that positive emotions act as a shield that protects you from challenges you may face with negative emotions.

Negative emotions constantly remind you of your problems. Think about it: whenever you started feeling anxious, most of the time, it was because you remembered something unpleasant or you thought of a problem that you would have to deal with later. Now, this doesn't mean that when you focus on good emotions, you become oblivious of issues. No, it isn't the case!

Don't focus your entire attention on the problem for too long, enough to get you upset, anxious, or afraid. With more emphasis on negative emotions, you would think that every day is horrible. You would think that you do not have anything to be grateful for at the end of it.

When we spend time to think about the effect of positive emotions and what complete reliance on it does to our health, we start to appreciate life more. We become open to conversations around being more positively driven.

You're Body on Positive Emotion

Scientists have been studying the positive effects of emotions for as long as they've been studying the negative effects, and it is generally found that people who experience more positive emotions tend to be healthier and live longer. When we feel more upbeat and positive, it causes our bodies to become better balanced, and our autonomic systems (especially the autonomic nervous system) function properly without the interference of stress hormones and other physical consequences of negative emotion. When we experience positive interactions with others and ourselves regularly, we provide our body with a cycle of balance and health.

Chapter 7: How to change your emotions

Assessing your emotional state is a key step in honing emotional intelligence as well as having empathy in general. Some people may be constantly cued into their emotional states, while some others may go a day or a week without thinking about it at all. Although it may be easy to fall into the trap of generalizations on the subject of the sort of people who think about their emotions and those that do not, the issue is not as straightforward as it may seem.

People who report that they think about their emotions frequently may be characterized as the sensitive, empathic sort. These are the type of people who naturally ask others how they are feeling, or who encourage others when they hear the news that suggests that the other may be going through a trying time. Some people naturally recognize their emotional state, and this can lead them to be sensitive to the emotional states of others.

Why do emotions often take control of people?

People don't Recognize Own Emotions as a Staging Ground

Recognizing your own emotions is the staging ground for then recognizing the emotions of others. This is why empathy and emotional intelligence do not consist of single emotional skills, but several of them. This should lead people to understand that successful emotional intelligence involves tying several emotional steps together for the goal of interconnectivity. If all you are doing is recognizing your own emotions, then you do not understand the emotions of others, and you are ultimately not behaving with emotional intelligence.

Therefore, recognizing one's own emotions is a starting point for behaving with empathy towards others. Indeed, recognizing individual emotions alone does not directly lead to sympathy, empathy, or emotional intelligence within us. If men and women focus solely on recognizing their own emotions but do not care about the emotions of others, then they are behaving with narcissism, which is the antithesis of the empathy that this seeks to encourage.

People don't know how to control feelings

Our feelings are expressions of our emotional and mental state of existence. Normally tied to our physical and social sensory feeling, they are used to react to joy, fear, love, disgust, sadness, hate, pleasure, and a host of other emotions. In other to prevent extreme behaviors which usually comes at high costs, we must control and suppress some emotions and feelings.

Persons who cannot generally control their feelings engage in unwarranted acts of violence, fighting, unprotected sex, and abuse of different substances which will undoubtedly put their lives at risks. There is a wide range of factors that contributes to such lack of control apart from the feelings generated by the mind. These factors include environmental, genetically, social, and biological factors.

People don't understand the impact of Emotions

There is an active connection between how you feel and the physical problems you experience, and this is because you are not different from how you feel. Most of the challenges you experienced in the past or the ones you are facing now have solid connections with your dominant emotional pattern.

When emotions are used in the right way, they can become a tool for empowerment, and when they are misused or repressed, they can become a gateway to suffering. A lot of people are afraid to maintain a positive emotion for a long time. They have accepted the mistaken idea that life cannot be so exciting enough for anyone to be happy all the time.

Of course, life has its moments, but this doesn't mean you should deliberately shut down positive emotions by not feeling it. If you embrace the positive sides of emotional experiences, you will be giving it the liberty to flow through your body. Most of the time, when you feel tired, it is because you are stressed out or have been thinking about something negative.

When your body is relaxed, it means that you are in a happy place and that your emotions are balanced. Don't try to control your emotional responses because you think it cannot be fun and joy all the time.

You need to start dealing with your emotions so that you can identify and get rid of the negative ones while embracing the positive ones.

All these discussions we are having about feelings and problems are so important.

Change your behavior and your bad habits

Feelings, especially intense feelings, can often are autonomous, which means they are automatic and subconscious, developing as the result of an external force or trigger.

To take control of our emotional selves, we must learn the signs of emotionally unstable people.

Denial

Denial is the refusal to accept the truth of a situation, and in short-term use, it is a healthy and effective coping mechanism. It allows the unconscious mind to deal with the situation before the conscious mind must deal with it. Persistent denial, however, can cause severe emotional distress; we all know that ignoring a problem will not solve it. Denial prevents us from dealing with our emotions and seeking support because we cannot face the issue at hand. It is so powerful; you may not even realize you are in denial until someone else helps you see it.

Being Overly Serious

Being too serious detaches you from your coworkers and friends. Nobody wants to say something funny they found online to you, because they would come off as not serious. You unknowingly miss out on the beautiful things in life, and it might begin to reflect on your family and kids too.

Going through Your Phone in the Middle of a Conversation

This is a very disrespectful act that is unfortunately very common nowadays. Some people are so attached to their phone that they can't bear to take their eyes off of it for an hour; hence they tend to go through their phone even when an important meeting is going on. This can mess up your relationship because it makes the person think you're insensitive. Bringing out your phone and going through it in the middle of a conversation is not only insensitive, but it's disrespectful too. You're telling the person that whatever they were saying to you, as important as it was to them, is unimportant to you, and that can make the person feel insignificant. You should stop using your phone in the middle of a conversation.

Calling the Names of the Important People You Know

If you cannot go through a conversation without mentioning the names of the important people you know, this is you trying to make yourself look better than every other person sitting in that room at that moment, and you do not necessarily have to drag that kind of attention to yourself. You have met the president—nice. Your father's brother is the one on TV—yeah, that's nice. Not everyone needs to know. Instead of making you look interesting, you come off as a braggart in want of attention and that sincerely puts people off. Name dropping might make you feel better about yourself, but how do you think it will make others feel about you?

Subtle Bragging

Subtle bragging, or humble bragging, is the act of bragging in a way that is not exactly noticed as bragging. You don't realize you are bragging when you practice humble bragging, because by your standards you are just modest. This is something we do among friends, sometimes innocently.

Screaming at People

No one likes a screamer. No matter how much the person deserves your screaming, it's not necessary. You make people feel small and insignificant when you scream at them. Especially when it is a constant habit of yours to scream when you are mad at others. You can say that it's just your way of reacting when you're mad, and that screaming makes you feel a lot better, but have you ever stopped to consider how the other person feels about your screaming?

Gossiping

When you gossip about another person, it says more about you than it does about the person you were talking about. It doesn't make sense to base your discussion on the life of another; relationships that thrive on gossip have a very shaky foundation and are bound to crash sooner than later. Gossiping is a horrible habit, and it depicts a very low state of emotional intelligence.

Talking a Lot More Than Listening

When you talk more than you listen, it limits your chances at learning and unlearning things. You are shoving your opinion down the throat of others without giving them the time or the chance to air theirs.

Listening most times helps you to make a better decision. Not listening to people when they talk and being too concerned about airing your own opinion will make you look ignorant. At some point, you will begin to say things that do not make a lot of sense because you were not listening in the first place. You will suddenly begin to look ignorant, and no one wants to associate with an ignorant person who is also not willing to learn.

Posting Too Much of Yourself on Social Media

A lot of people are guilty of this action. It depicts a want for acceptance, and it's usually captured by the phrase "putting it all out there." Well, news flash, you do not have to do this. You do not necessarily have to tell the world all the dreams you have or all the things you do after you wake up and before you go to bed. You do not need to be validated by social media and those online. They don't care that much about you. They should not know so much about you. It's needless throwing these things in their faces. Save some information for yourself. Remember, the internet has a good memory; it never forgets.

Saying Too Much of Yourself Too Early in a Relationship

Not everyone needs to know all the information you spill to them when you are talking to them for the first time. Sharing too much too early makes you come off as an attention seeker. It seems like you want the person to think you are real and open and want them to like you almost immediately. It's a lot better to let the relationship flow organically, and then the rest of the information will come out naturally without stress. It's also better to relax and try to know the other person better while trying to build trust in the relationship. Sharing too much of yourself is rushing things and does not give the other person a chance to be comfortable in the relationship.

Being Closed-Minded

This is a huge problem. It is important that you view things with an open mind. Keeping a closed mind makes you unapproachable. It also means that you already have a formed opinion about a certain thing, and when you are approached, you are unwilling to listen and make changes to your initial thoughts, making you inaccessible. It's very sensible to keep an open mind and be open to changes. These habits are associated with people with low emotional intelligence, and they should be stopped now. They are harmful to you, to the people around you, and the growth of your emotional intelligence.

Avoidance

Avoidance is similar to denial, but it is much more conscious. It happens when we cope with certain events, emotions, or thoughts by avoiding them altogether. For example, a person experiencing high levels of work stress may stop showing up for work. We avoid stressors in hopes of eliminating that stress, but this causes more stress and more discomfort because we are not dealing with the emotional trigger.

Social Withdrawal

Many people experiencing emotional turmoil will withdraw from family and friends. This is not to be confused with simply needing some alone time, which we all need sometimes. Social withdrawal happens when we feel too exhausted, overwhelmed, or insecure about being around people whose company we once enjoyed. Human beings crave connection, but it is easy to fall into withdrawal, increasing negative emotions like loneliness and self-doubt.

Compulsive Behavior

Compulsive behavior is the repeated engagement in an activity despite sense and reason, usually to the point of obsession. We engage in this type of behavior because it can provide temporary relief against negative emotions like anxiety, stress, and grief, but it can exacerbate these problems by leaving us feeling out of control of our behaviors. Examples of compulsive behavior include binge-eating, over-exercising, hoarding, gambling, and sex. For those struggling with Obsessive-Compulsive Disorder, these activities may seem very simple and insignificant, like hand-washing, checking (doors, gas taps, light switches, etc.), ordering/organizing, and counting.

Self-Destructive Behavior

Sometimes, we find relief from negative emotions through behaviors that are temporarily pleasurable but ultimately self-destructive. A great example of self-destructive behavior is smoking cigarettes despite knowing this habit can cause health problems later in life. We are often aware of the negative consequences of this kind of behavior, but we engage in it anyway for the relief it provides. Common self-destructive behaviors include smoking, alcohol abuse, drug abuse, binge-eating, and self-harm.

Change your environment to change

Under this view, individuals react to emotions in a personalized manner even though the emotions are universal. For example, when you feel upset, the way you react to the emotion will differ from the way your colleague reacts. The effect of reacting to each emotion in a personalized way is because of other influences on emotions. For instance, the resilience levels vary per person.

Additionally, the environment also impacts on the way we react to emotions. Think of how you react to bad news in public and when alone at home. It is necessary to review how one reacts to emotions using a subjective view.

In detail, various aspects of emotion impact the way we respond to it. For instance, the same emotion can have different intensity. An example may be where you feel happy, but the degree of happiness will differ per person in the audience. There is a possibility that an individual that has been enjoying positive emotions for the entire week not to feel the happiness being felt by others as intense. On the other hand, an individual that has been disappointed all along the week may find the happiness being felt by others as highly intense. The reaction to the emotion, in this case, will vary due to the intensity of the feeling of the emotion.

The subjective paradigm partially explains the complexity of emotions because each emotion is processed uniquely by each person despite the emotion being universal. The subjective paradigms appear to assert that focusing on making each person react uniformly to emotion is futile and instead the focus should be on generating the desired emotion rather than concentrating on how people will react to the emotion.

Chapter 8: How to deal with negative emotions

To get rid of all sorts of negativity from your life, it is important to build a positive state of mind. It is only when you become aware of your negative thoughts, challenge them, and constantly replace them with positive substitutes that you train yourself to control your extreme emotions and move past them. Here is how you can do this:

- Every time you find yourself catastrophizing the severity of an instance, reading too much into things, reducing someone who hurt you to a two dimensional label, and making negative predictions about things you do not feel too excited about, question the authenticity of those thoughts and emotions. For instance, if you see your friend losing interest in your conversation, and you jump straight to the conclusion that he/she hates you or no longer wishes to be your friend, hold on to that thought and question its genuineness. Ask yourself things like: Why do I feel that way? What proof do I have to validate my assumption? Has my friend always behaved like that? What about all those times when he/she was compassionate with me and listened to my problems patiently? Such questions help you come up with evidence that makes it easier for you to assess the legitimacy of your strong emotions and the negative thoughts that they stir. When you understand that you are merely thinking negatively due to your pre-conceived notions, you easily differentiate between healthy and unhealthy thoughts and can do away with the latter.

- Also, every time you think negatively about yourself or nurture a deep, negative belief about your capabilities, think of the emotion that stirred up those thoughts and beliefs and question their authenticity. If you feel you cannot win a competition, why do you think that is? If you believe that it is because you do not work hard then you know exactly what you must do to prove yourself wrong: work hard. It is important to find out the root cause of a negative thought and then address it in order to manage the negative thoughts and the underlying emotions causing them.

- Once you are done analyzing a negative thought or belief, find a more realistic and positive substitute of it and repeat it over and over again. For example, if you thought, 'I don't think I'll ever reach the break-even point in my business and forever struggle with improving the sales', change it to something along the lines of, 'My goal maybe difficult, but it is possible - especially if I work hard to achieve it.' Such realistically positive thoughts make you nurture hope and feel positive. Remember to chant it loudly repeatedly to imbed it in your subconscious mind. When you repeatedly focus on something, you activate your RAS (Reticular Activating System), which then perceives it as an important piece of information and sticks to it. Also, when you constantly think about something, you affirm it to your subconscious mind. When something is affirmed to your subconscious, it accepts it and slowly shapes thoughts in that direction. Hence, if you frequently feed positive suggestions to your subconscious and think about them day in and day out, you will soon get rid of all the unhealthy thoughts and emotions and replace them with healthy and positive ones.

You are capable of being happy, positive, and successful in life and that can happen only when you learn to replace negative thoughts with positive ones. It is natural to feel agitated, angry, and upset when things don't go your way, but you need to slowly train yourself not to hold on to those emotions, understand their implications, and replace them with more constructive ones by simply replacing ill thoughts with positive ones. To keep mastering your emotions, start working on overcoming your fears and anxious thoughts. The next chapter throws more light on this.

5 proven strategies and/or therapies to eliminate negative emotions and thoughts

Develop self-awareness

Self-awareness is about self-knowledge, about getting mindful of what is happening in your life, and about having an idea how you see your daily life or career developing. To be self-aware you need a certain degree of maturity and at least a vague idea of what you'd like to do with your existence. When you know what you want, it becomes easier to find a method of getting it. If you don't, you are left drifting aimlessly, with neither a goal nor a plan.

So, how can you develop self-awareness? Begin by increasing your sensitivity to your very own gut and emotions emotions, as they are generally the most trusted close friends you'll ever have. Make an effort to set aside a while for self-reflection, and think about your behavior, thoughts, emotions, frustrations, goals, etc.

Those who are used to self-analysis will find this easy probably, but if you're not used to this type or sort of thinking, this may be hard, even unsettling. In that full case, start by setting aside 30 minutes each night, once you're finished with the work for the day and may relax a bit, and think about the day or week behind you. If you had a difficult day/week particularly, ask yourself everything you can find out from the experience.

The purpose of this exercise is to truly get you used to considering how you feel and why.

Or, you may start journaling, and this is not about keeping a diary and covering your day-to-day thoughts and activities. Journaling is about recording any unusual or frustrating experiences, thoughts or emotions you might have had. Some things are not easy to go over with others, and anyway, not really everything is for posting, so why not get it off your chest by authoring it. The great thing about journaling is normally that to write something down, you need to believe about what to write; in fact it is often this technique of thinking about a problem that helps you see what's at the root of it. Therefore, if feeling upset, angry or disappointed, write it out and move on.

Understand your emotions and what triggers them

To comprehend your emotions you have to be willing to experience them. It's sad just how many people are afraid of their own emotions, especially negative ones, e.g. sadness, anger, bitterness, etc. and the moment they feel these feelings taking over, they perform something that may interrupt their train of thought, e.g. they could active themselves with something in order to distract themselves from these unpleasant emotions.

In the event that you recognize yourself in this, you should know that all you will achieve this way is postpone (perhaps indefinitely) facing your own demons and dealing with whatever it is that's troubling you. Feelings need to be experienced and dealt with, not buried.

Intelligent folks are not scared of their emotions emotionally. Whatever it really is they feel, they keep at it for so long as it requires for the emotion to end up being identified. There is a reason you feel how you do, and instead of ignoring them, you should try to "decipher" your emotions because they are trying to let you know something.

To become proficient at understanding others, you first have to be able to understand yourself. So, even the emotions you don't actually want to feel should be addressed, processed, and let go.

Listen without judging

Good listeners are uncommon, mainly because this involves a whole lot of empathy, willingness to give up your time and effort for others, and mental energy to be present when you are listening.

The primary trait of a good listener is to pay attention with empathy, and which means without judging. This is not easy always, and may in a few full cases be difficult, so if you understand you are biased towards someone, it's perhaps better not to talk to them in the event that you know you have already made up your mind about how you are feeling about what they are going to say.

So, to become a great listener you should attempt to be present during the conversation, and stay focused. This can be hard, as some social people don't stop talking, or have a problem stating what they mean so you may be looking at a few hours. However, if you are not interested in this person really, or you are in a rush, or are not feeling well, try to postpone the conversation for another time. The tell-tale indications of disinterest or boredom, e.g. glancing at your watch, or checking your cell emails or phone, can be extremely insulting and discouraging for the person you are having a conversation with.

Emotionally intelligent people show interest in others by encouraging them to speak even more (even if indeed they don't agree with what they are saying), and by creating a host where it's safe to start and say everything you really mean.

So, the next time you speak to a person who requirements your opinion, advice or simply a shoulder to cry on, try to be patient (some people have a long time to come to the point), focused (reserve this time limited to them and switch off your phone), and non-judgmental (provide them with the benefit of a doubt). By not becoming and judging open-minded, you might not only help the person by giving them an opportunity to obtain something off their upper body, nevertheless, you may also gain insight into what's going on in your team, or a family.

Also, focus on body language, both yours' and theirs', e.g. the modulation of voice, facial expression, body posture, etc. To a casual observer, these would be clear symptoms how you both feel about the conversation.

Active listening takes a complete lot of practice, but it is among those skills that you can practice every full day, of where you are regardless, and what it really is you are listening to.

Mind-Body Connection

This is about listening to the body and understanding what it's trying to tell you. According to the mind-body connection doctrine, irritation in a part of your body is definitely a sure indication something is not right. For instance, lower back discomfort is linked to financial problems, upper back discomfort to being overwhelmed with life, a knot in the tummy with nervousness or fear, etc.

Understanding how to notice these signals and interpret them, can help you save considerable time and difficulty with regards to understanding why you feel a certain way.

But, what frequently happens is that while your body is informing you that you are anxious, anxious, angry, or harm, you ignore these symptoms simply, hoping they would eventually go away.

Unfortunately, Western culture pays an excessive amount of importance to feeling happy and high at all times, so folks are not encouraged to deal with their negative feelings, but are advised to ignore them, e.g. by repeating positive affirmations, or repair them, by taking something that will make them experience better. Do you really believe that if you ignore your adverse feelings, do it again a mantra or take something to make you feel high, you will eventually become happy, confident, and fearless???

Sometimes, when you're overwhelmed with emotions, it may be OK to calm yourself straight down, in unhealthy ways even, until you may clearly think. But, this only gives temporary respite and is not a solution to your problem.

Emotional intelligence will help you get to underneath of your emotions by showing you how exactly to work out what the triggers are, and how exactly to interpret and release these emotions in the least harmful way.

Engage

How involved are you with your community? Do you volunteer? Is there someone you are helping with by moral support frequently, financially or otherwise? Are you there for others if they need you even though you know it'll ruin your weekend which you had planned to invest with your family?

Empathy is the primary trait of intelligent people emotionally, and it could easily be developed by anyone if they follow a couple of simple tips on how to develop or improve these abilities. But, the simplest way to develop empathy can be through practicing it. Put simply, whenever you engage with others, you are doing what emotionally smart people do: you listen, you try to understand, and you listen in.

Nevertheless, many people fake empathy due to the fact they'd like to be observed simply because emotionally intelligent. They say the right matter, are politically correct always, appear to be filled with deep empathy, listen thoroughly, offer help, etc. However, if caught off-safeguard or if for a few good reason not feeling in the feeling for putting up an act, their true character quickly comes out. Today, to advance professionally, if you see yourself as a head especially, you have to prove that you have high psychological intelligence, so those that fake it do that for self-promotion usually.

The easiest way to improve your empathy is to start taking interest in others, e.g. how they live, what's troubling them, how they cope, etc. Improve your listening skills and try to possess at least one deep conversation per month. By engaging with others, you automatically increase your emotional intelligence.

Develop self-management

Self-management is about controlling your emotions, not in the feeling that you suppress them or ignore them, but figure out how to deal with them, and only release them after you have processed and understood them. Self-management is also about being accurate to you. Some of the real ways you can improve your self-administration are through developing your integrity, e.g.:

- Practice what you preach

- Be prepared to speak up, even though you risk being made fun of

- Don't make promises you are unlikely to keep

- Continually be polite and respectful with co-workers, it doesn't matter how close you might be

- Be self-disciplined, especially if you anticipate that of others

Learn to cope with criticism

Negative feedback is usually often undeserved and a result of the person presenting it is not fully aware of your performance, or using the opportunity to sabotage your self-confidence perhaps, or undermine your job openly.

However, if truth be told, Atlanta divorce attorneys negative feedback there is usually a grain of truth. Although there might have been very good reasons why you underperformed or experienced a score of people complain about you, the truth is you failed. However, when you come to a stage when you're able to accept negative opinions, or open criticism, without taking it you demonstrate which you have both self-confidence and psychological intelligence personally.

So, how to become more open to negative feedback? Of all first, not all criticism is important equally, nor should you react to it in the same way. A colleague's remark about your brand-new hairstyle is actually a sign she's making fun of you, nonetheless it may be a subtle suggestion that the design doesn't suit you.

Besides, in the event that you receive less than satisfactory feedback on your own performance repeatedly, or behavior, instead of sulking or throwing a tantrum, try to look in yourself through other people's eye. Imagine if you ARE lazy actually, or short-tempered, or unreliable?

The key thing is to consider why you are feeling bad about the feedback. Is it because it's really undeserved and due to the person giving it devoid of a complete picture, or are you angry with yourself for not having masked your underperformance better? Or simply jealous others do better?

Admitting you were wrong isn't easy, but surviving in denial is even worse. So, than experience upset about the opinions rather, try to find out something from it. Especially if it's not the very first time the same thing has been brought to your attention.

But, regardless of how you feel, be aware that negative feedback, if given without malice, can perform more for your personal development, than can false praise.

Besides, there is something noble about admitting you had been wrong. It could not be a pleasant thing to do, but it teaches you are mature more than enough to take both the credit for your successes and blame for your errors. This may encourage others to do the same.

5 techniques to control the most important emotions such as fear, worry, panic, forgiveness, anger

One of the most important components of emotional intelligence is the ability to identify and manage your own emotions and other people's emotions. When you learn to observe your emotions and express them in a manner that is beneficial for the overall situation, you display high emotional intelligence. The unfortunate truth is that not many are adept at recognizing and articulating their emotions.

Sometimes, all we need to do to display high emotional intelligence is observe our emotions or feelings in a non-judgmental manner. The good news is, a person can increase his or her emotional intelligence by displaying a high understanding of his or her emotions through consistent practice. Here are a few tips for identifying or recognizing your emotions and expressing them:

Observe Your Feelings throughout the Day

Practice observing and identifying your feelings all day. How do certain experiences at various points in time during the day make you feel? When people say something that angers you, carefully note what exactly they've said to trigger the feeling of anger. This will help you develop a wide range of emotional vocabulary. I would even go a step further and say, for the purpose of quickly and easily identifying them, give your emotions names.

Labeling emotions makes it easier to identify specific emotions because even emotions like anger can have several different forms. For instance, it can be anger out of humiliation or anger induced by a feeling of jealousy or anger owing to expectations that are not met.

Naming your emotions makes it easier to identify and manage them. This practice also lets you take a step back from reacting impulsively and focusing on the cognitive parts of the brain for resolving issues. It will help you understand and make sense of your feelings more effectively. The practice gives you a better understanding of making choices when it comes to interacting with others.

You can note your reactions to events throughout the day in a journal as they occur. Avoid ignoring it because you're overlooking important information that can have a huge effect on your thinking and actions. Consciously pay more attention to your emotions and link them to everyday experiences.

For example, you are in a meeting, trying to make offers and suggestions, and a co-worker just cuts you off and takes the conversation elsewhere. What emotions do you feel at this point in time? Similarly, a few minutes later, your manager appreciates you for a task well done. What are the emotions and feelings you experience? When you get into the habit of clearly identifying emotions (and labeling them) such as anger, embarrassment, sorrow, elation, peace, contentment, envy, frustration, annoyance, etc., your emotional intelligence automatically increases. Start tapping into your emotions at specific points during the day. For instance, what is the first emotion you feel on waking up? What are the feelings you experience before falling asleep?

Practice Deep Breathing and Mindfulness

All our emotions are experienced physically. When we are angry, upset or stressed, the feelings manifest themselves through our body. Our bodies respond on an evolutionary level (instinctively or involuntarily) like they would respond to a natural threat. Some physiological reactions to our emotions can be a speeding heartbeat, increased pulse rate, sweating, shallow breathing and more.

When we calm down these physiological reactions, we quickly bring about a change in our feelings and emotions too. When you kill physical stress, the mental stress naturally melts away. Each time you find yourself feeling stressed or tensed, take a slow, deep breath. Focus completely on your breath and practice deep breathing. Pay attention to how it feels to have oxygen enter your lungs. Notice how your mouth, throat, lungs and abdomen feel when you breathe in and breathe out. Concentrate on the flow of air in and out of the abdominal cavity. Taking even a few deep breaths will make you feel better, and you will be in a positive frame of mind while interacting with other people.

Each time you find yourself diverting focus away from your breath, gently acknowledge the feeling without judging it and move the focus back to your breath. Stay in the present moment in a purposeful manner. Avoid thinking about the past or future and focus only on the breath. Your emotional frequency will change in no time.

Practice mindfulness (focusing attention on the present moment in a purposeful and non-judgmental manner) in all spheres of life to calm down your spirit (especially if you happen to be a more hot-tempered or easily irritable individual).

By practicing to observe your emotions and feelings in a non-judgmental manner, you not only boost your awareness of these feelings with greater clarity, but also reduce your chances of being overwhelmed by a bunch of negative or destructive emotions.

Question Your Perspective

The first step towards increasing your emotional intelligence and social skills is recognizing that there are multiple ways of looking at a situation. Even though you may completely believe that your perspective or way of looking at things is right, get into the habit of considering it from different angles rather than giving in to knee-jerk responses.

When you are angry or upset with someone, avoid reacting impulsively. Instead, slow down and consider various ways of explaining the circumstances. What are the different ways to explain the situation? Of course, you may still stick to your perspective but at least attempt to look at it from various angles before considering the situation in a calmer and more rational manner. At best, even if your perspective about the situation doesn't change, you'll get more time to calm down and think of a more positive, constructive response.

Celebrate Positive Emotions to Attract More of Them

Emotionally intelligent folks who experience greater positive energy lead more fulfilling relationships and are more resilient when it comes to responding to negative situations. Therefore, get into the habit of intentionally doing things that induce a sense of happiness and joy within you.

There are several ways to bring more joy into your spirit including performing random acts of kindness, practicing gratitude, being in the midst of nature, exercising, engaging in productive hobbies, creative visualization and reminiscing about past experiences that have brought you happiness. Celebrating positive emotions helps you attract more of this positive mindset, and it helps create positive experiences.

Know Yourself like No One Else

The epicenter of emotional intelligence knows you like no one else. Self-awareness is the key to developing greater emotional intelligence. Having a good understanding of your core characteristics, strengths, weaknesses, beliefs, values, attitude and other similar aspects of your personality helps you understand your positive and negative triggers.

You will understand what drives your responses and how you can manage them more effectively if you gain complete self-awareness. A person can gain higher self-awareness through personality tests, reflection, feedback from others and more.

Try to establish a link between your emotions and the actions or behavior resulting from those emotions. What drives your impulses? Which specific emotions spur you to behave the way you do?

Chapter 9: How to read emotions

By understanding how having emotions ties into the many aspects of emotional intelligence, we can healthily approach the subject. Some of the stigmas that come from so-called emotional people are that people that have been labeled as emotional may not engage in the associated steps of understanding other people's emotions, self-regulation, and empathy. This was touched on in the discussion of narcissism, but those who healthily embrace their emotions also embrace the emotions of others and know how to regulate their emotions if they begin to get in the way of social interactions.

This perception has to do with the idea that thinking about emotions too much is something negative. These dysfunctional perceptions have led to some people eschewing in any emotion, while others have taken the opposite side and have become advocates for emotion and emotional thinking. But this is a downward spiral that results from terminology not being used appropriately in the case of emotion. Showing compassion for someone is a sign that you feel emotion. All religions are infused with emotional feeling, and people become better friends, better family members, and better lovers because they care.

Emotion is the basis for meaningful social relationships. Having emotions does not mean that you are bogged down by them, which is how some characterize the term. By rejecting emotion or mischaracterizing emotion, we create a society where people either have distorted emotions because they do not understand them correctly or they feel no emotion at all because they have been taught to be wary of emotion based on misconceptions about emotion.

Coping with destructive emotions is rarely simple and rarely easy. You can begin to identify your repressed emotions by listening to the body. When dealing with repressed emotions, especially anger and rage, the body is often as affected as the mind. Repressed anger can cause chronic pain as well as other emotional turmoil like high anxiety and depression.

Overall wellbeing isn't just about emotional and mental health; it's about physical health, as well. Your physical and psychological selves do not exist separately. They are constantly interacting with one another. Keep reading to discover how your poor emotional health may be negatively affecting your body and your physical wellbeing.

Knowing how our minds work is part of the greatest mysteries we are yet to solve. A lot of individuals have dedicated their entire lives to understanding the mind, sadly to no avail. Understanding the roles of our mind and emotion to our well-being is paramount as it puts us in the driving seat in controlling our lives. This is simply a little part in our quest to use the mind in controlling our feelings but is one that must not be neglected. Similar to the relationship held by every part of our entire make-up, ignoring the interactions between our minds, emotions, thoughts, and feelings means we will be ignoring their roles. On a more serious note, this might be an aspect that we need to get fixed before taking further steps.

The mind and body do not function independently. They are not separate systems, and this can be observed when we are tensed. An instance of a moment of nervousness is a job interview or a first date with our long-time crush. Regardless of how calm and confident, we would like to appear in such instances; we discover that we are both tensed and self-conscious at the same time. The muscles of our buttocks will be tightened as a result of the self-conscious feeling we are experiencing. We sweat more than usual, and might even feel nauseous in such events, not forgetting those periods we would fluff our lines when we desire or attempt to be confident.

Our emotions which are constructed by the subconscious and highly influenced by the unconscious layer of our mind are what add value to our thoughts. For instance, let us say you were raised to believe that tipping a salt shaker over is a sign of bad luck. When you observe someone tipping a salt shaker unintentionally or do so you, your mind sends thoughts which project emotions.

Our feelings are expressions of our emotional and mental state of existence. Normally tied to our physical and social sensory feeling, they are used to react to joy, fear, love, disgust, sadness, hate, pleasure, and a host of other emotions. In other to prevent extreme behaviors which usually come at high costs, we must control and suppress some emotions and feelings.

Managing your emotions can be likened to developing a skill. It involves learning a better way of doing something. It requires change on our part. In reality, we struggle to accept change as humans. This is largely due to many factors, but the working of the mind is highly influential in this regard as we have discussed earlier in part one of this book. Controlling your feelings will get you mentally stronger. The good thing is, everyone can benefit it from controlling their feelings. Here is why you should keep your feelings in check.

Keeping your feelings in check is not the same thing as managing them. Ignoring how you feel about a certain situation will not make these feelings go away. Rather, such feelings will get worse when they are not addressed properly with time.

Create a Room in Your Life for Joy!

Being conscious of what positivity can do for you isn't enough. You've got to be intentional about it by creating room for the right activities that will help you achieve great emotions. People often ask how they can build joy in their lives, and I must say that one of the ways to do that is by connecting with the right people.

If there are positive and happy people within a circle of friends, the joy will be contagious, such that even when one person feels the tiniest form of anxiety, it will be cut off immediately. Your mental health receives a boost every time you connect with positive vibes from the right people.

Being around positive people doesn't mean your problems fly off the window, and everything is sunshine and rainbows again. It just means that you realize that there are issues, but you love yourself too much to allow the problems to steal your joy.

You've got to have a list of all your priorities. What is most important to you? Health? Wealth? Give attention to whatever matters the most to you. If you are all about gaining good health, then you must be deliberate about being surrounded by the right people while investing in quality emotional interactions.

Meditation is an essential tool that can help you stay connected to positive emotions. Think of negative emotions like a lot of noise that has no meaning yet drains you of your health and physical wellness. Positive thoughts, on the other hand, thrive in meditative sessions where your mind is at peace, and you are not distracted by toxic emotions.

Your ability to take control of your emotions will determine the kind of experiences you have with your health and the good feelings it generates within you.

Listen to Your Body

If your body is trying to tell you something, don't ignore it. It can be too easy to attribute physical discomfort to normal bodily changes, like aging, when, in fact, your physical symptoms may be caused by your emotional turmoil. It is also important to notice when pre-existing conditions worsen for no physically identifiable reason. Chronic stress and anxiety can wreak havoc on our bodies when we are coping with other illnesses.

Connect with Others

The professionals who study the physical impact of negative emotions have found that there is a direct link between perceived positive connections with others and improved physical health. The more we have good social interactions, the better we are at manifesting positive emotions within ourselves, and vice-versa, which relieves the body of a lot of physical stress. If we can maintain this "upward spiral dynamic" between positive emotion and positive social connection, we can more easily grow in our emotional selves and therefore improve our physical health.

Practice Relaxation

Another great way to counter the negative physical effects of intense negative emotion is through the practice of relaxation. When we actively relax, it allows for all the natural processes that can cause harm within the body (like fight-or-flight) to turn off or reset, providing relief from stress hormones, muscle tension, and other physical symptoms. The practice of meditation is an effective and therapeutic way to practice relaxation.

Analyze Your Response

When you turn to face your negative emotions, take the time to analyze them. Ask yourself, "Is this reaction appropriate to the scale of the situation? Does this emotional response offer me anything? What can I do to make this situation better? How can I learn from this situation to respond better in future situations?" Using your mindfulness practice is very important to this step. By getting to know our emotional selves better, we can better understand and change our emotional responses.

Practice Breath Control

When you are experiencing an intense negative emotion like anxiety, fear, or anger, take a deep breath, and try to take slow, controlled breaths while focusing your attention on your breathing. This act can help to lower blood pressure and slow an elevated heart rate. You may count the number of breaths you take if you're having trouble focusing. Practicing breath control is an important part of many stress-relieving practices, such as yoga, tai chi, and meditation.

Letting go of your emotions

Emotions are energy in motion, but what happens when you prevent the energy from moving? It accumulates. When you repress your emotions, you interrupt the natural flow of energy.

Sadly, nobody taught you how to deal with your emotions or even that both positive and negative emotions, are a natural phenomenon. Instead, they told you that your negative emotions should be repressed because they are bad.

As a result, you may have been repressing your emotions for years. By doing so, you let them sink deeper into your subconscious, allowing them to become part of your identity. They have often become patterns you may be unaware of. For instance, perhaps, you feel you aren't good enough. Or maybe you experience guilt regularly.

These are the results of core beliefs you developed over time by repressing your emotions.

Most of us have too much emotional baggage and need to learn to let go of it. We need to declutter our subconscious and get rid of the negative emotions preventing us from enjoying life to the fullest.

How to Condition Your Mind for Better Emotions

One of the effective ways to condition the mind for better emotions is to handle impulses. Most emotions are expressed in an impulsive form. Letting emotion express full always seem fulfilling as it lets out the emotional energy within a short time, allowing the status quo to be restored. The author argues that handling impulses are the best approach to conditioning the mind to realize better emotions.

Managing Impulses

An impulse refers to a sudden thought that is overwhelming. An impulse is an irresistible urge or emotion. Handling an impulse will require purposely seeking to enhance or depress the intensity of emotion, including committing not to act on a desire. The critical skills for handling an impulse involve decision and control of where you focus attention to. Remember that our emotions emanate from our thoughts, and this argument implies that learning to control our thoughts will lead to the effective management of the emotions. Learn to focus to or away from particular thoughts as a strategy of handling impulses. It can be argued that learning to make a decision and managing where you direct your attention to will lead to improved management of impulses.

Correspondingly, one should learn to stop the urge to act on a desire. Arguably true, you should develop emotional awareness, including social awareness. There are several ways to accomplish control of impulses, and one of the ways is to develop emotional awareness by maintaining a journal of specific emotions and how you responded to it. By having a journal of the frequent emotions and how they express, one can develop an intervention that tries to stop the trigger factors that spur that emotion. For instance, if you feel irritated on certain days and you can determine the underlying causes, then it is best to manage those factors rather than managing the subsequent reaction. The urge is to let out your entire anger while the argued intervention is to discourage your mind enjoying full control of the emotion.

Chapter 10: How to use your emotion to grow

Emotions and Finances

On the positive side, certain emotions can make it easier for one to take risks. People that can process negative emotions and show moderate positive emotions may take risks and invest in the stock market, for instance. For one to take risks, he or she must be mentally prepared for both positive and negative success. In other terms, one must exhibit the ability to handle negative emotions and recover in good time. People that have a positive outlook are likely to take risks even when the market is not performing to expectations. If you feel energized, feel confident, and feel hopeful, then taking a risk and investing is not a big deal. Marketers understand this and will invest time in eliciting the right emotions before inviting you to buy their stock.

Emotions and Love

Exhibiting positive emotions may make you more lovable. In nearly all cases, showing positive emotions makes one highly relatable, and this makes the person more lovable. Try to reflect on your school days or workplace and note which people you prefer. Showing positive emotions may attract more people around you. There is a high possibility that you prefer a person that shows happiness, hope, and is motivated over a gloomy person. Since emotions can be infectious, positive emotions may spur positive feelings from the other person.

While positive emotions are desirable, it is counterproductive to bottle up negative emotions in the quest of wanting to attract admiration and love. All emotions are necessary and should be expressed.

Emotions and Personal Success

Managed emotions, both positive and negative, can enhance personal success. In this context, personal success involves having fruitful social interactions, social relationships, and better financial management. On the positive side, emotions positively affect relationships and personal life management, which enhances personal success. Think of an individual that is motivated, happy, and resilient. The person is likely to also relate well with others.

Emotions and relationships

For emphasis, improving your emotion can help in relationship management when one has to be assertive. There are a lot of misconceptions about assertiveness as some people think it projects one as domineering, selfish, or rigid. Assertiveness is important as it helps communicate boundaries and your position. Assertiveness does not imply not listening to others or being inflexible. In this manner, assertiveness in a relationship can be a source of friction when one or both of the parties does not acknowledge the idea of assertiveness. An example is where an individual is trying to assert her opinion and the other person misconstruing that to mean that the former's opinion has to prevail at the expense of others. However, with emotional intelligence, one can perceive the reactions of the other person and take into consideration when asserting personal views.

Furthermore, improving your emotions is likely to make it easier for you to resolve conflicts with others with success. In life and especially at the workplace, conflicts are unavoidable due to the unique nature of human behavior. Most contemporary workplaces are diverse, and this increases the risk of conflicts. Diverse workplaces may see conflicts arising from cultural insensitivity, stereotypes against sexes, race, religion, and socioeconomic aspects of other workers. All of these contribute to making a workplace a depressing sight. If each employee could recognize their emotions, it becomes easier to make others aware of how they feel and this can make it easier to prevent a conflict.

Chapter 11: The key to control emotions

Generally, people consider anger management to be about anger suppression or repression. But, it is not about that at all. It is not a healthy choice to never express your anger. In fact, anger is a healthy emotion which you should always express when necessary or justified. No matter how hard you try to suppress anger, you will always show the signs. And, anger only becomes volatile when you have held it in for so long.

The goal of anger management is to help you understand where your anger is coming from and the underlying emotion behind it so that you can find ways to express it without losing your cool. When you know the place your anger is coming from, you not only find it easier to express this anger healthily, it also strengthens you so that you can manage your life and relationships better.

Mastering your emotions to achieve anger management requires a lot of patience, diligence, and practice which means you must be willing and ready to put the hard work in. Once you achieve your anger management goals, the results can be pretty rewarding and fulfilling. With anger management, you can build and develop better relationships, improve your mental and physical health, chase you dreams, achieve you goals, and ultimately improve the quality of life you lead.

The first step in anger management is **identifying the cause or trigger of your anger.** What makes you angry? Is your anger a standalone emotion or is it a substitute for another emotion? Or, maybe it is even a secondary emotion which stems from another related emotion? Ask yourself: "what am I really angry about?" Look deep within yourself and your situation to identify the real source of your anger. If you have ever gotten into a big fight over something really little, it must have left you feeling really silly and you must have wondered what was wrong with you at a point. So, take time out to search within you and try to identify that cause. Is it some other feeling like shame, fear, or insecurity? Are you so angry because of some trauma from childhood or were you subdued as a child? Maybe your anger is even a learned behavior? In some cases, your anger may also be due to situations out of your control or certain people in your life. However, this doesn't mean you should pin the blame of your anger on other people. It is more to do with learning the exact source or trigger so you can work on it, whether it is a person, past experience or current situation. Once you learn the source of your anger, it becomes very easy to move on to the next step of anger management which is to recognize your anger warning signs.

How do you tell when you are about to experience a sudden anger outburst? You **become self-aware of the preceding signs** before you lose control and get all angry. Many people feel that anger is an immediate emotion like you can just explode into anger without a forewarning but it doesn't work like that. Before a violent angry outburst, your body gives you some physical warning signs that you need to start looking out for. Becoming self-aware and recognizing the different signs your body gives before explosive anger is crucial to anger management because then, you can learn to tame your anger before it goes out of your control. Some of the telling signs you may have right before an anger episode are;

- Faster breaths
- Knots in the stomach
- A flushed feeling
- Tightly clenched jaw or fists
- Pounding heart
- Tensed muscles and shoulders
- Lack of concentration
- A detachment from logic and understanding

Once you recognize your anger telling signs, the next step to take is to **determine if the bridling anger is a friend or your enemy**. There are angers you need to express and those you need to tame and put under control. You should always express any anger that seems like a friend and keep the one that seems like an enemy under topnotch control. Before you take steps to calm yourself down after recognizing some signs of a coming anger, determine what kind of anger you are about to express. For instance, if you just witnessed someone being assaulted, you immediately feel a sense of injustice and your brain confirms to you that this is an unhealthy situation which shouldn't be happening. With the sense of injustice come feelings of anger which can be helpful in the situation. So, in this came, you don't try to calm yourself or change your emotional state, what you do is use your anger as a motivating factor for doing something to change the situation. Anger sometime gives us a much needed courage to stand for a change or initiate one. However, if you sense that the coming anger is one that makes you feel excessive distress and discomfort or makes you want to lash out at something or someone, then you know it is an enemy and you have to prevent it from taking control or consuming you. In this case, you work on the emotion triggering the anger to calm yourself down.

Use effective anger management techniques to calm yourself immediately you sense a pending outburst of anger. Once you become self-aware of your anger warning signs, you can start using some anger management strategies to calm yourself before the storm. It is easier to tame your temper when you are already familiar with your anger triggers and signs. There are different techniques you can try out to help you maintain you're cool and keep anger at bay. Here are some strategies you can employ to manage your anger;

- Concentrate on the physical sensations your body gives when anger starts brimming. Although this may seem like counterintuitive techniques, it can actually be pretty helpful. Focus on your physical sensations by tuning into the very feelings your body gives when you start getting angry; this can reduce the intensity of the anger you feel and alter a possibly instinctual or impulsive reaction

- Take some deep breaths, slowly. A very deep slow breathing exercise can be helpful in countering tension in the body. The idea behind a breathing exercise for releasing tension is to take a deep breath right from the stomach, making sure you take in as much air as possible into the lungs.
- Take a quick walk or any other physical activity. When you are faced with an anger-triggering situation, going for a brisk walk can help you avoid expressing the anger the wrong way. Physical activities and exercises helps release the built-up energy which otherwise may be used to lash out unhealthily at a person or object nearby. This can really help calm you so you can approach the situation with a cooler version of yourself. For example, if you get in an argument with your spouse and you can feel your anger bridling, simply tune into your emotions and take a walk from the situation so you can calm yourself down. Of course, this may be challenging to do but with resilience and regular practice, you will get better at taking that much needed walk away from self-destruction.
- Tune into your five senses for quick stress relief to release the tension and knots in your muscles. Your senses of sight, hearing, smell, taste, and touch can all be used to activate immediate stress relief so you can calm your mind and body. You can tune into your senses by stretching the areas of tension, stroking a pet or something

dear, listening to your favorite music, or savoring a great cup of coffee.

You can also manage your anger better by devising or finding healthier outlets for releasing pent-up anger. Devising healthier means to express feelings of anger is key to successfully master your anger because like we have said, you aren't meant to hold your anger in. If you think a situation is really unfair, unjust, or wrong, the one thing you can do to change this situation is to find healthier and non-destructive ways of expressing the induced feelings of anger. As long as you have healthier means of expressing your anger, also keep it in mind that you should know when to let go. If you can't come to an agreement over a conflict even after expressing your anger, ensure you know when to draw the line and move on from the situation or person who is the source of the anger.

Communicate your feelings with a trusted person. Talking to someone you actually trust is a great way of easing stress and letting out the feelings you may have bottled in. This person does not need to have answers to your questions or solutions to your problem; simply talking to them can provide an instant relief from stress and anger. Communication in this context does not mean venting or lashing out verbally; it is more about talking about your feelings and seeking a fresh and entirely new perspective to whatever situation is on ground. Venting will only reinforce your anger not decrease it.

The last course of action in anger management is to **seek professional help** especially when you know that your anger isn't something you can work on by yourself. There are times when anger management strategies and techniques are simply not enough. In this case, you can go for an anger management class where you can meet people with similar anger problems and learn tips for managing/controlling your anger from a trained anger management professional. You can also go for either individual or group therapy so as to explore the source of your anger and identify the possible triggers. Therapy is a very safe place for expressing all of the emotions you have bottled inside you. It is also a great place to discover new healthy outlets for expressing feelings of anger.

Before you express your anger in any situation, ensure that a calm demeanor is already achieved and you are in the position to approach the problem from a level-headed angle.

How culture impacts emotions

Culture also has a huge role in determining how we perceive, experience, and responds to our emotions. The culture in which you live has laid-down rules, guidelines, expectations, and a structure to help you understand, interpret, and express your emotions within an acceptable context. Based on where you live, there is probably a standard for the accepted degrees of emotional display. Culture dictates how you experience or react to negative emotions; there are guides to help you regulate how you react to emotional triggers. Different cultures appropriate different contexts to different facial expressions and as we have said, there are theories which believe that our facial expressions are cues for the emotions we may be experiencing.

Culture is the values, beliefs, and behaviors that make up the way of life of a set of people and it can also profoundly impact your perception of emotions and reaction to emotions. Cultural display rules influence how you experience emotions by providing rules to regulate your emotions. For example, in European culture and a place like the United Kingdom, individuality is highly promoted while many Asian cultures such as China promote social harmony not individuality. This means someone from any part of Europe is more likely to express their negative emotions both with others and on their alone while a Chinese is less likely to express their feelings in the presence of others. So, a person from a culture that encourages social harmony is more likely to be the emotion-repressing type because they always try to evaluate the right response which fits the socially acceptable structure and guideline.

Again, every culture has certain consequences ascribed to the expression of different negative emotions. There are cultures where expressing a negative emotion like anger can cause you to be socially ostracized. In the United States of America, a man could be socially ostracized for crying in the presence of others. Cultural norms also impact how both genders perceive and display emotions. Studies in the past have provided evidence to show that men and women may experience and display emotions differently based on some socio-cultural guidelines. Culture also impacts how emotions are interpreted, either by you or the object of your emotion. Cultural contexts influence how we interpret facial expressions of emotions. People who come from different cultures will likely interpret the same facial expression in entirely different ways.

Although our cultural contexts impact how we experience and display emotions universally, emotions are universal because all humans have the ability to recognize and make facial expressions. The seven universal emotions which we will always experience and display no matter our culture are: happiness, sadness, anger, fear, surprise, contempt, and disgust. These emotions have the same meaning across the universe but our culture and cultural display rules will profoundly impact the responses and reactions we give to these emotions either as an individual or a society.

Chapter 12: Famous and motivational speeches

Imagine that you're standing in front of your staff members during a meeting, giving a speech that's supposed to motivate them, but you see several bored and confused faces in front of you. You don't want to bore your audience; a great speech motivates, educates and provides information. A moving speech is one that's emotional and tells a breathtaking story that makes a positive impact.

Most of those who attended the meeting may forget about your message. First, you want to know and understand your staff so you can tailor your message to them. This involves researching their likes and dislikes, their needs and desires, their goals and struggles, their personality types, and their strengths and weaknesses. This is where your staff profile cards will come in handy. Review their profile cards, cross-reference their mutual motivation triggers and link them to your story and goals. You don't want to speak for yourself; you want to speak on behalf of your staff.

They should believe in your message and to feel motivated by it. If your speech is tailored with them in mind, then they're more likely to remember your message.

Remember that even though you're the only person who's speaking; create a two-way conversation with your staff. Imagine yourself developing a relationship with your workers even before you show up at the meeting. Successfully connecting with your staff all comes down to having confidence in your message and understanding them. You want to craft your message into something they understand so they can improve on their job skills.

When creating your motivational speech, your goal is to come up with one major point, so you don't confuse your staff members. Have you ever listened to a speech and walked away wondering what that person was even talking about? This is an issue you want to avoid. Your staff should get valuable experience out of your speech. Respect their time and attention by emphasizing the main point of your speech, but remember that having too many messages are just as bad as having none.

Make ensure that your speech keeps your staff members engaged throughout the meeting. If you educate them in a genuine and engaging way, it'll build upon that relationship you already have with them. They'll know who to turn to whenever they need your influence or inspiration, and they will respond accordingly.

Each speech must have a beginning, middle, and an end. It's the key to storytelling. Your staff members will engage with you best if you let them know what the speech is about and include guideposts along the way. You want to explain how you arranged your speech, including the main points. Spend extra time on each section, so you can determine the right verbal cues to use so your staff knows where you are in your speech. You don't want to lose your audience's interest.

Your staff can tell the difference between leaders who's passionate from one who has no interest in what they're saying. Remember that you're telling them an incredible story they never heard before. Even some of the most boring topics can sound amazing if it's told by a leader who's excited about this topic and sounds like a storyteller. Being passionate can prevent your speech from sounding stale. Since speeches allow you to be creative and passionate, you want to prevent boring your staff members to death.

Keep those notes in mind when writing your speech before each meeting. Practice making everything better with several rewrites and practice and you'll craft speeches that your staff will remember for a long time. Check the resources section for a template to build upon and more examples.

Key Points:

1. Know your staff.

2. Connect with your staff.

3. Focus on one main point.

4. Educate your staff.

5. Have a good structure.

6. Express your passion.

Throughout history, many excellent orators have delivered memorable speeches that created a huge impact on a lot of people's lives.

One of them is Civil Rights activist and church minister, **Martin Luther King Jr.,** who delivered his now-classic **I Have a Dream** speech, on April 23, 1963. The piece is regarded as the greatest speech of the 20**th** century.

King begins by mentioning part of Abraham Lincoln's Gettysburg Address, which is the foundation of his cause. The Emancipation Proclamation that was signed a century ago by then President Lincoln still stands today. MLK describes its signing as **"a joyous daybreak to end the long night of their captivity."**

MLK Jr. likens the promise of freedom to an unpaid debt. He believes that their forefathers' promise to all men (blacks and whites alike) of life, liberty, and happiness will still be fulfilled. The Emancipation Proclamation was supposed to have given the African-Americans equal rights, but even after a century later, they were still considered as second-class citizens in America, and this was what ignited the fire that MLK kept burning all his life.

He reiterated that all men, regardless of their skin color, have equal **rights to Life, Liberty, and the pursuit of Happiness.** This was guaranteed by the Constitution and the Declaration of Independence

As he continued, he did so without referring to his prepared speech, but spoke from his heart. This is the most quoted and the most memorable part of his speech.

The ability to project confidence in everything one says and does requires multidisciplinary effort. We know from experience that people tend not to follow individuals who are not confident in their own words and actions. Subconsciously, we perceive them as weak and unfit to lead, even in the smallest capacity. As people tend to be extremely susceptible to the aura of the outward appearance, great leaders have always been aware of the importance of how they present themselves. The multidisciplinary nature of confidence involves hand gestures, facial expressions, body posture, and tone of voice, breathing, speaking pace and so much more. Importance of public perception cannot be overestimated, which is why people in leadership positions have teams of advisers who work with them on their public image.

Recent research into the relation between leadership and narcissism suggests that leaders can become more effective with the practice of humility. By dealing with one's ego and not being self-centered, the positive narcissistic attributes like confidence, vision and persistence can be seen in practice. True leaders have the confidence and stamina to face challenges and make tough decisions. Confidence improves social aptitude and helps create long lasting relationships. Leaders who are sure of themselves tend to be happier and more positive.

They take more risks and think creatively with a deep sense of their personal values.

Perhaps one of the best examples in political history demonstrating the importance of perceived confidence in the public eye was the 1960 US Presidential election. Political historians explain that at the presidential debates, which for the first time were broadcast on live TV, Kennedy's relaxed and confident posture and talk made the decisive difference against Nixon's tense and seemingly uncomfortable television appearance. Kennedy's confidence portrayed him as the more suitable leader in the eyes of the people.

The Signature Symbol

Abraham Lincoln is not thought of as a president who nurtured his image. But why did this six-foot, four-inch figure of a man, who towered over his contemporaries, choose a stovepipe hat as his signature symbol? It only accentuated his height. Plus the long shawl he wore draped over the shoulders of his dark suit enhanced the lankiness of his frame.

FDR's cigarette holder, Churchill's cigar, and Stalin's pipe—these were familiar symbols during the World War II era. The statue of Winston Churchill in front of the British embassy has the wartime prime minister holding a cigar in his hand. On the other hand, the recently dedicated Franklin Roosevelt Memorial in Washington is a disservice to our Depression and World War II. President Franklin Roosevelt is shown seated in a wheelchair. Instead of the jaunty, buoyant smile that people of my generation remember from photos and newsreels, Roosevelt's face seems tired and taut. Absent is the cigarette in its holder, which the "politically correct" removed.

The Roosevelt Memorial Committee also chose to reinforce the disability theme by featuring the famous sayings of Roosevelt in braille (but so far up that even basketball player Shaq O'Neal, if blind, could not reach to touch them on tiptoes!). Curiously, FDR's most famous line, "a day that will live in infamy," from his Pearl Harbor address, does not appear in the twenty presidential quotations cited on the memorial.

FDR's Invisible Wheelchair

The seniors among us never saw a photograph of Roosevelt in a wheelchair. Roosevelt, who understood Power Presence, never allowed a camera to photograph him in a crippled state.

In 1924, when Roosevelt was to deliver his speech on behalf of Governor Alfred Smith for the Democratic presidential nomination, he arrived at an empty Madison Square Garden early enough to position himself in a chair behind the lectern. Four years before, Democratic Party delegates had witnessed a healthy and robust Roosevelt, whom they chose to be vice presidential nominee on their ticket with Governor Cox of Ohio. There was no way Roosevelt was going to let them see him enter in a wheelchair. When the time came for him to speak, he propelled himself in a leap and grabbed the lectern. During the applause that greeted him, a gasping Roosevelt had time to collect himself from the draining effort. A Power Presence was all-important for Roosevelt.

Power Accessories

Winston Churchill knew the impact of Power Presence. His "power attire" was a navy blue pinstriped three-piece suit with a gold watch chain he had inherited from his father bisecting the vest. He usually chose a blue polka dot tie that brought out the color of his eyes. The cuffs of his white shirt bore gold links with the Marlborough crest. A crisp white handkerchief flared from his lapel pocket.

Churchill, like Roosevelt, was a born actor. He knew the power of his props: the heavy black-rimmed glasses he donned for reading his speech, the cigar he waved with his left hand, and the "vee for victory" sign he flashed from his right hand. Even his hat was distinctive—a hybrid of homburg and bowler, custom made by Locke's of London.

Maggie's Handbag

The second greatest British prime minister of the last century was fanatic about her appearance. For Margaret Thatcher, no week went by without her bouffant coiffure being lightened and touched up. Her tailored suits—either solid violet, navy blue, or forest green—were immaculate and ever adorned with an exquisite brooch pinned to her left lapel. She was a star and played the role. Beside her, her male ministers looked drab. She appointed no female to her cabinet. She liked to be the only woman in a room or in a photograph. With her handbag and carefully modulated voice, she had the presence of a schoolmarm or nanny presiding over her charges, the other British politicians.

CHURCHILL KNEW THE POWER OF HIS PROPS: THE HEAVY BLACK-RIMMED GLASSES HE DONNED FOR READING HIS SPEECH, THE CIGAR HE WAVED WITH HIS LEFT HAND, AND THE "VEE FOR VICTORY" SIGN HE FLASHED.

Conclusion

Emotions are predominantly sited in the unconscious implying that we have significantly less control of how emotions occur. It is for this reason, that body language is critical in determining the true status of an individual as the unconscious impacts much of the body language. With all these developments, emotions are highly manageable. The book emphasized consistently that the focus should not be on preventing emotions but allowing them to manifest safely. Most people have the wrong assumption that negative emotions should not be expressed forgetting that emotions are a form of energy, and they need to dissipate.

We hope that after reading the book, you'll understand why those with higher emotional intelligence have a better chance of being successful professionally and feeling more accomplished personally.

Your path to success depends on many things, but mainly on how well you manage to navigate your way through life. Developing emotional intelligence can help you stay on course.

You'll keep experiencing negative emotions throughout your life, but, hopefully, each time you'll remind yourself that your emotions are not you and will you will learn to accept them as they are before letting them go. You're not sad, depressed, jealous, or angry; you are what witness these emotions. You are what remains after these temporary feelings fade away.

Your emotions are here to guide you. Learn as much as you can from them, and then let them go. Don't cling to them as if your existence depends on them. It doesn't. Don't identify with them as though they define you. They don't. Instead, use your emotions to grow and remember, you are beyond emotions.

Made in the USA
Las Vegas, NV
27 October 2022

58275141R00079